hidden **territories**

'The achievements of Gardzienice come as a wonderful gift . . . one of the few essential theatre companies working anywhere in the world today.' *Susan Sontag*

'One of the world's premier experimental theatre companies.' *Richard Schechner*

Hidden Territories: the theatre of Gardzienice is the first full-length articulation by Włodzimierz Staniewski of his philosophy and practice. This remarkable theatre director, with collaborator Alison Hodge, gives a fascinating insight into his company's principles and techniques. The text is accompanied by a unique collection of photographs drawn from the company's archives.

This innovative publication is a landmark in the documentation and appreciation of contemporary performance. The PC-compatible CD-ROM which accompanies the book enables the reader to experience the stunning visual and aural complexity of the performances through extensive video footage of productions, rehearsals and training in full colour. The CD-ROM also includes key essays, photographs from the Gardzienice archives, performance scripts, director's notes and a full chronology of the company's activities.

Włodzimierz Staniewski is the Artistic Director of the Centre for Theatre Practices 'Gardzienice' which he founded in 1977. Gardzienice's performances have since established the company as one of the world's leading avant-garde theatres. **Alison Hodge** is a freelance theatre director and senior lecturer in Drama at Royal Holloway College, University of London. She has collaborated on a number of projects with Gardzienice since 1989, and is also the editor of *Twentieth Century Actor Training* (Routledge 2000). **Peter Hulton** is the director and founder of Arts Archives which has produced five series of videos and CD-ROMs documenting the work of international practitioners. He is a senior research fellow at Exeter University.

hidden **territories**

the theatre of gardzienice

włodzimierz staniewski
with alison hodge

cd-rom produced by arts archives

 Routledge
Taylor & Francis Group

LONDON AND NEW YORK

First published 2004
by Routledge
11 New Fetter Lane, London EC4P 4EE

Simultaneously published in the USA and Canada by Routledge
29 West 35th Street, New York, NY 10001

Routledge is an imprint of the Taylor & Francis Group

Book © 2004 Włodzimierz Staniewski and Alison Hodge
CD-ROM © 2004 Włodzimierz Staniewski

Typeset in Joanna by RefineCatch Limited, Bungay, Suffolk
Printed and bound in Great Britain by TJ International Ltd, Padstow, Cornwall

AUTHORWARE® COPYRIGHT© 1993, 2000 Macromedia, Inc.

British Library Cataloguing in Publication Data
A catalogue record for this book is available from the British Library

Library of Congress Cataloging in Publication Data
Staniewski, Włodzimierz.
  Hidden territories : the Theatre of Gardzienice / Włodzimierz
Staniewski with Alison Hodge.
    p. cm.
Includes bibliographical references.
  1. Stowarzyszenie Teatralne "Gardzienice" – History.
2. Theater – Poland – History – 20th century.   I. Hodge, Alison, 1959–
II. Title.
  PN2859.P6S67   2004
  792'.09438'0904 – dc21   2003011584

ISBN 0–415–26297–6 (hbk and CD-ROM)
ISBN 0–415–26298–4 (pbk and CD-ROM)

contents

illustrations

preface

Hidden Territories is the first full account Włodzimierz Staniewski has given of his theatre practice and the philosophical and aesthetic principles that inform it. The text is the result of a series of discussions that we conducted between 2001 and 2003. The original document was in the form of a dialogue. On reflection, I abandoned this discursive style in favour of a monologue, which provided a greater fluidity to the text. However, in one or two instances my questions or comments have been retained where their further amplification of an issue seemed useful or necessary.

It is worth noting that this book has been spoken rather than written, and in a form of English which is idiosyncratic. In an effort to retain the sense of Staniewski's voice, I have kept his choice of words wherever possible.

The book is divided into five major sections. In 'Origins', Staniewski offers an introduction to his theoretical ideas in relation to his practice. In 'Practice', Staniewski describes the company's field work – the expeditions and gatherings – which establish the context for his performances. In 'Technique', he elaborates on the principles of musicality and mutuality which inform both his actor training and performance aesthetic. In 'Performance', Staniewski selects three of the productions and discusses their ideological sources and dramaturgical development. In 'Conclusion', Staniewski considers the future form and function of theatre.

A CD-ROM accompanies this book. It contains footage of the performances, and also explores the environment and the processes that surround and inform the work, including Gardzienice's training, rehearsal and performance spaces, the village, expeditions and gatherings. Additional material includes photographs of Gardzienice, critical essays and reports on performances, performance scenarios, director's notes and explanations of training practices, and a full chronology of all activities undertaken by the ensemble between 1977 and 1996.

The opportunities opened up by basic multimedia technologies such as the CD-ROM allow a more dynamic engagement between the reader, the text and the visual and aural nature of the work. While the text and the CD-ROM can be used independently, they are designed to enlighten each other, and the reader is invited to explore this relationship in his or her own way.

Alison Hodge
London, 2003

acknowledgements

We are extremely grateful to the Arts and Humanities Research Board for their financial support in developing this project and to Małgorzata Szum and the Polish Cultural Institute for their assistance in translating a number of articles. For permissions to publish articles, we gratefully acknowledge the following: Leszek Kolankiewicz, Albert Hunt and Peter Hulton, Halina Filipowicz, Richard Schechner and Bronisław Wildstein. Every effort has been made to contact copyright holders. Where this has not been possible, we would be pleased to hear from the parties concerned.

We would like to thank the actors and directors who contributed to the making of the films included on the CD-ROM and whose names are to be found on the credits on the disc. On behalf of Peter Hulton we would also like to acknowledge the invaluable assistance of Kevan Williams of the Learning Development Unit, University of Central Lancashire, and Dorinda and Anna Sky for their inspirational support.

Finally, we would like to thank Talia Rodgers for her faith in bringing this project to publication, Dan Rebellato for his encouragement, Anna Dąbrowska, Paulina Brzezińska and Joanna Holcgreber for their work on the photographs, Jane Bell for her generosity, Dagmara and Irja Staniewski for their support, and Hannah and Sophie Hurford for their patience. Without Peter Hulton the CD-ROM would not have been possible and we are indebted to Chris Hurford for his unfailingly good advice.

introduction

Włodzimierz Staniewski has been the Artistic Director of Gardzienice Theatre for more than twenty-five years. His work has led the company to worldwide critical acclaim and has placed him at the forefront of contemporary theatre practice. Richard Schechner considers Gardzienice as 'one of Poland's – and the world's – premier experimental theatre companies . . . [They] constitute the very heart and essence of Polish experimental and anthropological performance.'[1]

From their base in a small village in southeast Poland, Staniewski and his ensemble have created their Centre for Theatre Practices, restoring the annexe of a seventeenth-century manor house, a chapel, the village mill and several cottages. The restoration of the village buildings has come to symbolize the ethos of Staniewski's larger vision: to build a 'theatre from the ruins', from the marginalized and diverse heritage of Poland's indigenous peoples. In practice, this research has inspired Staniewski's development of a new stylistics of musical theatre.

Staniewski's theatre has been described as 'ethno-oratorio', a unique song theatre inspired by the expressive traditions of indigenous culture and the musicality of the natural environment.[2] It simultaneously engages with many of our contemporary concerns – such as ethnicity, identity and ecology – whilst refuting what Staniewski views as the dispassionate quality of much postmodern art. Somewhat heretically, he also insists on the basic human urge for personal and collective transcendence through theatre – a heightened state more familiar to tribal cultures than to the audiences of what Staniewski calls the 'administrative theatres' of modern societies.

Gardzienice's international success is not solely based on the strength and depth of the group's musical and physical abilities, nor in the coherence of the performances' intellectual themes. Their work would also appear to be truly populist, recognized and appreciated by isolated rural communities around the world, from the Indians of the Taos Pueblo, New Mexico, to the Hutsuls of the Carpathian Mountains in Ukraine. At the same time, their performances cause an often powerful resonance within sophisticated urban audiences at theatre festivals worldwide. The critic Halina Filipowicz notes that 'Gardzienice's work does not necessarily transform lives, but the memory of this experience may force some to develop capacities for perception and understanding that were previously dormant.'[3]

Beginnings

Włodzimierz Staniewski was born in 1950 in the small town of Bardo in southwest Poland. The historian Norman Davies has described the Communist leadership of the time as having 'led their country [. . .] from the ruins of war to the ruins of the communist peace' (Davies 1984), and Staniewski's adolescence was spent in what he experienced as its repressive atmosphere. Whilst graduating in humanities from Kraków University he joined one of the country's leading student theatres, Theatre STU. Like many such groups in the early 1970s, Theatre STU combined political engagement with aesthetic experimentation.[4] Staniewski appeared in three of their devised productions, including one of the group's best-known performances, *Spadanie* (*Falling*).

Drawing on a poem by Tadeusz Różewicz, *Spadanie* combined literary texts, fragments of reportage and political statements to present a radical theatre which was an 'indirect critique of the Polish socio-political situation' (Cioffi 1996: 114). Staniewski has described this early experience as 'a crucial initiation into theatre' although he acknowledges that in his work with Gardzienice he has not pursued such an overtly political thesis. He points out that the intention of STU's work was to comment on reality, 'and I also wanted to show reality as it was. I wanted to open the curtain to the theatre of the world that officially didn't exist' (Staniewski 2002).

Crucially, *Spadanie* was a musical piece. According to a contemporary critic 'music is part of the staging, it shapes the movement, creates not only the atmosphere . . . but it is in competition with the word in establishing the dynamics of a performance' (Szybist 1982: 53–4).[5] The aesthetics of Staniewski's own theatre, founded on musical principles and incorporating textual montage, began to be formulated during this period.

In the same year, Staniewski was invited by Jerzy Grotowski to join his Laboratory Theatre in Wrocław to participate in the group's paratheatrical programme. At this time Grotowski had moved away from performance towards a more intimate process of communication and exchange, seeking to break down the barrier between audience and actor. A series of work sessions were conducted by members of the Laboratory in which the public were invited to participate in ritualized encounters. Frequently occurring outdoors and using the natural environment as a resource, these semi-improvised exercises intended to offer a process of self-discovery for those who participated:

> Grotowski's post-theatrical work explicitly shifts the locus of meaning away from its conventional place in the perception of the spectator, relocating it . . . in the experience of those who do. The basic impulse of the work is autotelic, concerned with performative elements as a tool by means of which the human being can undertake a work on her/himself.
>
> (Schechner and Wolford 1997: 11)

Staniewski collaborated closely with Grotowski, living in the rural environment of Brzezinka and conducting workshops at home and abroad. Interestingly, his contribution to the work appears to have been significant: the Laboratory's literary director, Ludwik Flaszen, has implied that amongst Grotowski's collaborators within the Laboratory, and despite his comparative youth, Staniewski 'was leading the most important experiences. He was the most advanced of us all' (Allain 1997: 49).

Gardzienice's emphasis on the interaction with the environment, the extreme physicality of its actor training and its integration of the artistic activities with daily life indicate some clear parallels with Grotowski's own practices at this time. But there were also significant differences of approach, and after five years of collaboration the two practitioners followed separate paths. While Grotowski had abandoned the theatre of representation, Staniewski wished to refocus on theatre-making: 'something with its own performative architecture, possessing more than changing rituals and ceremonies' (Staniewski 1987: 159). In 1976 he moved to the city of Lublin, and began to explore a very public theatre in the Polish villages, in contrast to the increasingly intimate atmosphere of Grotowski's Laboratory conditions.

Into the villages

Lublin is the capital of the deeply rural and ethnically mixed region of southeast Poland. Here Staniewski began participating in workshops and collaborating with various groups such as the student theatre Scena 6. However, by August he had found a disused chapel in the village of Gardzienice, 60 kilometres (40 miles) from the Soviet border, and here he gathered an initial group to form the Gardzienice Theatre Association. Of his early collaborators, Tomasz Rodowicz and Mariusz Gołaj (who joined in 1979) have remained with Staniewski to the present day, and have been intrinsically involved in the development of the ensemble's practice – Rodowicz focusing on the musical work, and Gołaj on the physical training of the actors.

For the first twenty years the basis of the ensemble's research was the 'expedition', in which members of the company travelled to remote rural villages in eastern Poland. Here the dominant Catholic communities co-exist with more marginal Gypsy, Belorussian, Łemko and Ukrainian cultures. Travelling on foot, the group spent a few days in each village, meeting with the local musicians and artists, exchanging songs and stories.

Staniewski glimpsed in these communities what he later called a 'new natural environment of theatre'. The Gardzienice actors began to gather material orally from the villagers, while presenting their own songs and fragments of performance in return. This process of what Staniewski terms 'naturalization' enabled the ensemble to develop the material amidst those who had originally inspired them, and whose own critical responses tested the integrity and impact of the evolving work.

The avant-garde tradition

Gardzienice's theatre practice can be positioned in relation to the broader context of the European avant-garde, whose modernist ethos includes the notion of a primitivism that could return Western theatre to its origins:

> If the present is seen as too sophisticated, rational, materialistic, technological, or repressively Christian, then 'the primitive mind' is taken to exemplify the naive, the irrational or sexuality. It embodies the spiritual, in harmony with nature, or representative of pagan freedom. Ignoring the diversity of native cultures, the 'primitive' is generally imagined as a universal quality: the quintessentially human from which European history has deviated.
>
> (Innes 1993: 16)

In its intercultural ambitions (as exemplified by Artaud's appreciation of Eastern theatre forms) the avant-garde has consistently upheld an interest in older forms of theatre and traditional cultural practices. At worst this has resulted in an exoticism where the deprivation and diversity of native cultures are ignored in favour of a utopian image of homogenous tribal traditions. Intercultural practices remain problematic. As Chin notes, they hinge on

> the question of autonomy and empowerment. To deploy elements from the symbol system of another culture is a very delicate enterprise. In its crudest terms, the question is: when does that usage act as cultural imperialism?
>
> (Chin 1991: 94)[6]

As part of their intercultural experimentation of the 1970s, both Eugenio Barba and Peter Brook undertook their own expeditions to indigenous cultures. Both practitioners were developing work which drew on performance traditions other than their own to create what Pavis refers to as a 'hybrid' form of theatre. Jerzy Grotowski, with whom Barba studied in the Laboratory phase of his work, had also drawn on Eastern techniques in his actor training in the 1960s. Like Barba, Grotowski's interest became increasingly transcultural in its

intention to 'find specific elements of performance that transcended
the particular cultures in which they were embedded' (Schechner
2002: 244).

In the mid-1970s, Staniewski was also seeking inspiration from
indigenous cultures, but his interest lay in the rural and folk traditions
of his own country, which had been largely forgotten and ignored
by the Communist authorities. Staniewski's early expeditions had
both socio-political and artistic intentions. The government had pro-
moted an idealized image of rural life, a version of folk culture which
ignored the diversity of peoples and the hard conditions in which
they lived.

Refuting this notion of a common culture, Staniewski's expeditions
and subsequent gatherings publicly recognized the underlying pluralism
within these Euro-Asian territories. In seeking his own inheritance, he
began to explore the multiple aspects of his own culture – historical,
ethnic, geographic and artistic. In this, Staniewski was not hampered by
the restrictions of language and his group was able to establish direct and
immediate contact with the people of the region. Cioffi describes the
members of the group coming to a village, 'to sing, dance, and eat with
the inhabitants, more like sons and daughters returning for a visit than
like scientists' (Cioffi 1996: 208).

Staniewski rejects what he called 'the modernist dogma [that
proposes] folk culture as an arcadia where art has its roots'. Instead,
he finds a more volatile environment, which 'presents man's inner
freedom, unfettered force, the world of laughter, continuous creation of
forms, their polyphony and dialogues', which offered 'a great potential
for theatrical dynamism'.[7]

Staniewski was already familiar with the work of the Russian cultural
philosopher and Rabelais critic, Mikhail Bakhtin. Formulated in the
Stalinist era, his theories of carnival and grotesque realism were directly
explored in Staniewski's first performance. Bakhtin proposed a dynamic
world of opposites in which 'terror was turned into something gay and
comic. Folk culture brought the world close to man, gave it a bodily
form' (Bakhtin 1965: 39).

The early performances

In their early expeditions to the villages, the group presented fragments of their training and performance work based on Rabelais's *Gargantua and Pantagruel*. Developed from this initial process, their first performance, *Spektakl Wierczorny (Evening Performance)*, was presented in 1977.

A combination of high and low culture, grotesque oppositions and subversive inversions were key elements to which Staniewski referred in Gardzienice's early work. In the outdoor space, lit by burning torches, the actors sang both religious and popular songs, performed acrobatics and joked with the crowd, kissing the women which, according to Filipowicz, caused 'shrieks of laughter'.

> The performance speaks more to the senses and emotions than to the intellect and reason. There is no storyline or development, only a quick succession of brief and dynamic episodes. The organising factors are fast-paced rhythm and a dazzling interplay of opposites.
>
> (Filipowicz 1987: 62–3)

The reactions to the provocative episodes were diverse, as Włodzimierz Pawluczuk observed:

> The audiences enjoy the Gardzienice group's performances as long as they watch without becoming aware of form and pondering their meaning. But when they do, they often do not like what they think they see. The leaping flames in the middle of the night, supple half-naked bodies and the often coarse text . . . give an impression of watching something sinful.
>
> (Pawluczuk 1981: 52)[8]

Another important influence on Staniewski's fieldwork was Julius Osterwa, whose Reduta Theatre toured Polish villages extensively during the 1930s. Osterwa's vision of a company of artists that should serve society through their artistic activity led to a rigorous, communal life in which the group constantly sought to develop their skills. As a close admirer of Stanislavsky, Osterwa placed much value in the training of his actors, and established an acting workshop and school. He died in 1947, but his approach inspired the work of a number of Polish practitioners, including both Grotowski and Staniewski. Gardzienice's theatre shares Osterwa's values in various aspects of its work, particularly in the emphasis on process and the continually evolving 'line of life' of each performance. This is developed through meticulous training and a close mutual exchange with communities which Osterwa believed reflected the deeply 'inter-human' nature of theatre.

After presenting *Spektakl Wierczorny* in the villages, the Gardzienice ensemble found that the audience would often stay and sing: 'Singing was the most open channel of communication [. . .] We saw ourselves facing a tradition that had always existed' (Staniewski 1987: 141). It was this tradition that Staniewski now sought to explore, and the key to this process was what came to be known as 'gatherings'.

Gatherings were semi-formal meetings arranged in the villages' communal spaces. Here the Gardzienice members would sing and perform extracts of a performance, while the local people would play instruments, sing, tell stories and dance in response. George Hyde notes the inclusive nature of this process:

> Less exclusive than Grotowski, more far-reaching than Osterwa's theories, Gardzienice extends the workshop principle into the community, making the culmination of any series of performances a full communal activity, drawing on the skills, crafts and trades of the village, as well as their folklore, songs and symbols.
>
> (Hyde 1992: 206)

Staniewski describes these gatherings as 'proto-theatre' which 'stands at the dawn of each cultural tradition'. It became Staniewski's theatrical reference point, as he emphasizes in Chapter 6: 'If you observe the traditional gatherings in the villages . . ., you will see that they are richer and more developed than many dramas done on the stage.' Through working and living on the apparent periphery of central and eastern Europe, Staniewski had found what he believed to be a 'new, natural environment for theatre'.

Polish Romanticism

Many of Staniewski's ideas were forged in the persuasive fires of Polish Romanticism, and in particular his fascination with Poland's rural folk traditions can be considered in relation to the ethnographic ambitions of Poland's greatest Romantic poet, Adam Mickiewicz. The invocation of the departed ancestors in a pagan ceremony becomes, for Mickiewicz, 'the model for theatre as a sacred rite' (quoted in Gerould 1986: 1). In his classic work, *Forefather's Eve*, this ceremony provides the structure for a semi-autobiographical, dream-like text which traces the political awakening of a young Polish man. Mickiewicz's political and poetic form demonstrated the eloquence of ancient Slavic folk culture as a means of reconnecting with Poland's cultural identity.

By the early twentieth century, Romanticism had been largely discredited in the West as an aesthetic retreat from harsh reality – what David Blayney Brown calls a 'compensating revolution in hearts and minds, an alternative empire of the imagination' (Brown: 2001: 11). However, the Polish movement continued to flourish under a series of repressive regimes, producing in its theatre a plethora of aural and visually complex styles – new theatrical languages through which to avoid censorship and undermine the State's authoritarian values. Staniewski's ideas were forged in these persuasive fires of Polish Romanticism. Behind his search for ancient and diverse cultures is also a search for identity, necessitated by its shattering loss in the oppressive years of foreign occupation. For Staniewski, whose first forty years were spent under Communist rule, the question of identity remains critical.

Sorcery and *Avvakum*

Gusła (*Sorcery*), first performed in 1981, was based on fragments of Adam Mickiewicz's *Forefather's Eve*, interwoven with Russian and Belorussian songs. The influence of Rabelais was still evident in the 'profane' language and carnivalesque elements of folk imagery, but Staniewski had also begun to incorporate sacred images and symbols from Christian and Chassidic traditions, and in particular the whirling ecstatic dances of the Chassidim:

Sorcery created an intense reality that was rendered unreal [. . .] full
of dissonance and tensions, songs and dances, shouts, whistles,
moving processions, flights heavenward, sensual desire, magical
spells, incantations and a maddening whirling.

(Taranienko 1997: 397)

By now Gardzienice were already touring abroad as well as performing in the villages. In 1983, *The Life of the Archpriest Avvakum* fully
elaborated Gardzienice's style of song theatre and consolidated their
international reputation. In the forty-minute performance, pagan rituals
and Russian Orthodox songs again combine with extracts from
Mickiewicz's *Forefather's Eve* and from the biography of Archpriest
Avvakum, the fervent leader of the 'Old Believer' Orthodox movement
who was excommunicated and burned at the stake in 1682.

Avvakum was made under the authoritarian conditions imposed by
martial law. Somewhat audaciously, given Moscow's dominant influence
in Poland at that time, Staniewski turned his attention to the traditional
Russian archetype of suffering as expressed by this persecuted martyr.
Presented as an ambiguous figure, the Archpriest is revealed as both
sinful and saintly in his defiance of the church authorities. Staniewski
describes the performance as 'an exploration of the Russian soul'. For the
critic Halina Filipowicz, *Avvakum* offered an image of estrangement:

> *Avvakum* shows a culture directed towards a moral ambiguity and
> latent despair. It stresses the indeterminacy of the stage world and
> thus reflects a parallel uncertainty of values, morals, and social norms
> in the world of the spectator. It is a meditation on an unsuccessful
> struggle toward spiritual life, on human isolation and homelessness
> [. . .] a view of human existence as eternal wandering in search of
> a lost spiritual homeland rather than a journey or a pilgrimage to a
> destination.
>
> (Filipowicz 1987: 161)

For other critics, *Avvakum*'s complexity offered a multifaceted experience
which could not be reduced to a single interpretation:

> The effect of this variegated and exhausting work was a presentation
> of uncommon intensity, of manifold meanings, quite impossible to

translate into the language of discourse, to capture in the form of an 'interpretation'. Despite the problems of exegesis, there is really no doubt that *Avvakum* is a masterpiece, and that Gardzienice ranks among the masters of contemporary theatre.

(Kosiński 2000: 23–4)

In the following years the ensemble toured extensively. Expeditions to indigenous communities further afield took members of the company to Lapland, Mexico, Brazil, Scandinavia, South Korea, Italy, Ireland, Ukraine, the Balkans and Egypt. It was increasingly evident that the training and practices that Gardzienice had developed in Poland were mirrored and affirmed by practices in other cultures, such as the form of mutual singing in Lapland known as *yoik*, and the ritualized running of the Tarahumara people in Sierra Madre.[9]

Attributes of love

In many ways Staniewski's fourth performance, *Carmina Burana*, marked a new phase in the ensemble's practice. First presented in 1990, it responded to the monumental social and political changes in central and eastern Europe brought about by the collapse of Communism. In Chapter 9 Staniewski describes the Polish reaction to the demise of totalitarian authority as euphoric: 'a huge emotional bundle of good feelings, wishes, dreams, beliefs, expectations – and all of these are attributes of love. We know more about the attributes of love than love itself . . . I wanted to deal with love.'

Staniewski chose one of the oldest European legends, the story of Tristan and Iseult. The fragmented narrative was driven by songs from the medieval collection known as the Carmina Burana, together with indigenous laments and folk songs. The piece marked a continuing shift away from purely Slavic and Orthodox sources towards a wider range of historical pan-European influences.

Carmina Burana is a complex essay on the vicissitudes of love. Staniewski used the symbolic depictions of love in the literary tradition of the Middle Ages to develop his own language of allegorical motifs. For example, in a striking visual metaphor, the stage was dominated

by a Wheel of Fortune, a huge wooden construction upon which
the actor playing Tristan was spun as the tragic disintegration of the
lovers' narrative took its course. According to the Polish critic Zbigniew
Taranienko:

> The space of *Carmina Burana* has become the place of the play of
> cosmic forces. Humanity has become entangled. 'The iconography
> of love' full of rapprochement, partings, yearnings, betrayals,
> reconciliation, fulfilment, admissions of guilt [. . .] entangles itself
> with its own philosophy of history, with the allegorically shown
> conception of the rise and fall of the kingdom of happiness, with the
> history of the destruction of the cosmic order.
>
> (Taranienko 1997: 400)

In addition, the performance was musically the most sophisticated
that Staniewski had so far attempted. Working with the philosophical
significance of musical ideas[10] Staniewski began to explore notions of
harmony and dissonance, reflecting the themes of the piece in which
love is depicted as a series of symbolic phases beginning with harmony
and ending in disintegration.

Antiphony, a responsive form of singing which is based on question
and answer, also became an important musical dynamic within the performance. In terms of Gardzienice's practice, antiphony reinforced those
aspects of their training which relied on the mutuality between actors:
physical, mental and vocal.[11] Through the ongoing development of
their intensive training processes, the actors' technical virtuosity was
becoming more closely aligned to Staniewski's increasingly eclectic and
resonant artistic vision.

Carmina Burana was an immediate international success, and positioned Gardzienice at the forefront of world experimental theatre.
The group continued to tour extensively while also responding to
the growing interest in their training methods, including a series
of workshops for the Royal Shakespeare Company in the UK from 1991
to 1995.

Metamorphoses

Since the early expeditions in the Polish villages, a key aspect of Staniewski's theatre practice has been the depiction of the dynamic contrast of everyday realism with a lyrical and even spiritual transcendence. In Chapter 3 of this book, Staniewski refers to Van Eyck's combination of mythic symbols and the everyday which creates a sort of mythic hyperreality. He outlines the way in which the artist

> depicts the world in which he was living, but at the same time, through inscribing mythical details and symbols, he suddenly achieves an astounding effect. He switches realism into transcendence. . . . We normally don't bring these ideas together. We see them as complete opposites. Why? I see them as neighbours.

In *Carmina Burana*, Staniewski explored the notion of the *coniunctio*, a potent alchemical symbol. It refers to the union of unlike substances resulting in a new material. For Jung, this conjunction symbolizes two poles of possibility within the psychic process which, if brought to the level of consciousness, can result in a transformation of the psyche.

The dramatic potential of this idea was more fully investigated in Gardzienice's next production, *Metamorphoses* (1998). Staniewski again drew on a popular folk narrative – Apuleius' *The Golden Ass*. It is the story of a search for the self, in which the hero is transformed into a donkey, discovering spiritual renewal through initiation into the Isis mysteries, before returning to his human form. In Gardzienice's performance, these trials dramatize the tension between degradation and sublime transcendence:

> This position is perhaps revealed on the stage in the most striking way, at the threshold of the sacrilegious. The actor (Gołaj) suffers as he finds himself placed on a pole that becomes his cross. He falls into orgiastic trance and transforms the cross into a huge mock phallus. However, in opposition to the overuse of such images today, these are in no way just cheap attempts to shock or provoke audiences. They serve as a dramatic expression of man's dilemma.
>
> (Wildstein 2002: A13)

Metamorphoses is a polyphonic piece that arose entirely from the inspiration of the music of ancient Greece. Staniewski acknowledges that the ensemble had to learn the music 'not from people but from stones' and the papyrus onto which the few remaining fragments of music had been inscribed. In order to reanimate this historical notation Gardzienice's composer, Maciej Rychły, incorporated them with the living folk music of Balkans, Greece and southern Italy in a process which Staniewski calls 'excavation'. Tomasz Rodowicz describes how every song was sung in different ways, 'from pathos to irony, from joy to hysteria. One has to do that to wake up its hidden energy or expose its emptiness.'[12]

In a two-part programme the performance is followed by a demonstration in which the process of excavation is explained by Staniewski and the ensemble:

> They ran slides showing fragments of writing on Greek vases and jars which have been translated into songs, then showed us with their own bodies how the two-dimensional movement of the human figures also depicted were transformed into the dances of their presentation. To say it was fascinating to observe and uplifting to the human spirit are both major understatements.
>
> (Holder 2003)

At the time of writing Staniewski is furthering this line of research, drawing on Euripides' *Electra* and developing a wider vocabulary of gestures inspired by the vase paintings of ancient Greece.

A life project

An important feature of Staniewski's theatre is its educational emphasis. This is seen as an essential and integral part of Gardzienice's practice, and has led to a large number of workshops, demonstrations, symposia and the establishment of a two-year course for Polish students at the Academy of Theatre Practice in the Centre. Here students engage in expeditions, vocal and acrobatic training, master classes, and contribute to the running and maintenance of the Centre. Every activity forms an integral part of the students' training. The relationship between their work and the natural environment is encouraged through outdoor activities and through the company's practice of 'night running', which aims to sharpen the sensibilities of the students prior to evening sessions. In Chapter 4, Staniewski identifies the importance of this form of education, which he believes encourages a more instinctive, mutual response:

> I am protecting the right to educate young people in the way that nature speaks to them. [. . .] the sources of creation are not only in the human mind. They are everywhere in living nature. It is only a question of being able to perceive, to see.

In emphasizing the interaction with the natural environment, Staniewski stresses the importance for the students to deepen their perceptual awareness and, by extension, their ability to respond instinctively within the dynamics of the partnership exercises and the close harmonies and dissonances of the vocal training.[13]

Staniewski consciously aligns this holistic outlook to the ancient Greek notion of *paideia*. Jaeger describes this form of education as 'a steady gaze that did not see any part as separate and cut off from the rest, but always as an element in a living whole'. Moreover, the Greeks' oral transmission of knowledge embodied the philosophical connection between sound and the notion of 'soul':

> They considered that the only genuine forces which could form the soul were words and sound, and – so far as they work through words or sounds or both – rhythm and harmony; for the decisive factor in all *paideia* is active energy.
>
> (Jaeger 1986: xxvii)

Staniewski's theatrical vision, which very determinedly seeks for those forces 'which form the soul', is extremely close to this philosophy. In Chapter 5 he observes the survival of traditional processes which combine both education and theatre to release a heightened level of perception that is rooted in the everyday:

> When in an indigenous village I see a grandfather teaching his grandson a song, gesturing the words and sounds and stamping the syllables, I think of *paideia*. A complex theatre. The grandfather

inscribes, his grandson reads the line of life of music, the line of life of the body and the word.

This statement is revealing in that all aspects of Gardzienice's theatre practice are underpinned by Staniewski's perception of musicality, which he defines in the book's central sections on the actor's technique. On a performative level, musicality functions as an imaginative catalyst, shaping Gardzienice's theatre language, replacing verbal discourse and releasing the narrative from a purely linguistic semantics to one of sound. The interweaving of text, gesture and song creates its own vocabulary, enabling the audience to read each element through the other within the careful orchestration of sound and image on stage.

Redemption

Reviewing a performance during the ensemble's tour of North America in 2003, Kathleen Foley suggested that:

> Those who dismiss avant-garde theatre as a sham perpetuated by the intellectually supercilious have never encountered this group. It's the real thing . . . bringing us as close to the divine essences of art and theatre as we are likely to get in this frictional, fractious culture.
>
> (Foley 2003)

The idea of humanity's fall and redemption are powerful Christian symbols. In Chapter 1, Staniewski makes direct reference to them in his discussion of the metaphor of Milton's lost paradise. This yearning for a utopian ideal is understood by Staniewski as emanating from a sense of alienation, a 'lost innocence' or tragic estrangement from the ground of our being.

Staniewski's practice seeks to overcome this through a form of redemption which he arrives at, not through divine intervention, but through a rigorous search for a deeper understanding of our contemporary selves. In the opening chapter he describes how his work attempts this by revealing the patterns of earlier cultures whose most potent traces can be found in homogenous societies:

You recognize one particular gesture as true because it has a genealogy that has existed for millennia [. . .] For me, it is a fact and the only stable reference point. The only one that keeps me in order. If we lose our reference points, we can forget about our lives. We will be like wandering, lost souls.

It is in these 'scattered pieces of truth' that Staniewski believes we will finally be restored to ourselves.

section one

origins

a thousand pieces

In a postmodern world there is no measure or scale of significance. We can create 'whatever', which helps us only in one way: it allows us to forget a sense and quality of the past. For this, postmodernism is perfect.

Why do we so desperately want to kill the past as our reference point? It has a certain logic, as in the beginning of Communism in Russia. Mayakovsky used the saying, 'The mare of history will charge to its death'. The Communists wanted to kill the past in order to build a 'brave new world', and we know how that ended . . .

Perhaps it is the same now: we want to build a 'brave new world' and, as usual, when you do something for the future with such determination, without any compromise, you want purposefully to kill the past. I think it is a very dangerous game.

Milton spoke of truth, saying how once it came into the world in a perfect shape, most glorious to look at, but now it is scattered into a thousand pieces. These words speak to me because they reflect the myth of a paradise lost. This memory, which is somewhere in our genes, tells us that once upon a time there was a perfect world in which everything was based on simple, clear, pure indispensable rules and ethics. It is necessary to remember that on the one hand it is a metaphor and on the other, in Milton's time, there were practical efforts to re-create, reinvent such idealism within society.

Milton speaks to me about the truth because he says that we have lost our stable reference points. At one time human beings referred to nature, its structures and its laws. Nature is no longer an ethical reference point. But if we don't have reference points we are definitely lost, we cannot create. Today everything is ambivalent and the way to make any sense is to create ambivalence. The truth is ambivalent. Salt does not signify salt, sugar can be salt.

The truth was scattered into a thousand pieces. We cannot look for one fundamental truth; nothing like that exists. You can look only for small pieces and try to build a mosaic.

In acting there is nothing like absolute truth. There are small elements which can be composed in different ways and each functions like an instrument to touch that which can be called essential. Some small gestures, some tiny sounds, the small steps of an old man going to the toilet in the morning. He goes there and back because he is always forgetting something: he forgets his handkerchief, then his soap, then his toothbrush and he is always on his way to his destination. But he is always forgetting something. He collects these essential elements, which, at the very end, compose an of act of destination which might reveal the truth. One of these thousand pieces, the broken mirror of truth.

It is necessary to search for these pieces. This task is a sort of conquest, like the quest for the Holy Grail. In searching for the Grail, one is somehow not looking for one permanent truth but searching for some remains of the lost paradise.

Theatre wouldn't exist if the world was perfect. Maybe theatre exists because the ideal, the tableau of the perfect world, was broken into pieces and theatre is trying to ask: Why did it happen?

Myth is the past and the past is myth. Myth is a complex image, a tableau. Agamemnon caused the death of Iphigenia, Clytemnestra killed Agamemnon, Electra caused the death of Clytemnestra. This is a complex image, a myth, a tableau. A mosaic of small pieces. A creator comes and asks these questions of the tableau: Why did it happen? How did the drama occur? Aeschylus, Sophocles and Euripides interpreted the myths introducing their knowledge, imagination, and the voice which they received from the gods, into myth. There they inscribed small pieces of truth − of gestures, of voice, of *peripateia* and built a model. At this moment theatre emerged.

Another tableau: A table, twelve people sit around it with the thirteenth in the middle; another complex image, another myth, another past. There are endless variations with which this event can be composed. A creator picks some small truths which are scattered around him and around us. The same then as now. And he or she builds a model which speaks to us as a perfect crystallization of the event.

Imagine you go to an old-fashioned theatre. The curtain opens and there is the first tableau and you think about a perfect model immediately. It doesn't matter whether it is provocative, obscure, obscene – the first picture is, for you, the model. It is like the first view, *thea*, meaning 'to see'. Then everything collapses, everything is broken into pieces as in Milton's metaphor. We know that the first five years of a child's life are very significant: all the tableaux the infant registers in its psychosomatics are like perfect worlds. Then, at a certain moment, when innocence is lost, the rest of life is a desperate attempt to try to rebuild small pieces of the destroyed tableaux.

I think that the Milton metaphor is still hopeful, because he says, 'Undertake your conquest. Make this effort now and try to find these pieces of truth. Do this impossible work and recompose it in your own way'.

Tragically, we are taught that the destruction, so often around us, is inevitable. The entire world is on fire. Everywhere something is falling apart, something is being destroyed and we are taught that there is nothing left. There are no pieces remaining. This is tantamount to saying, 'Get away from here, escape from this world, the faster the better'. What does it mean to escape? Like Sarah Kane,[14] to the dark side? Some do. For others, the so-called 'social engineers', the possibility of abandoning this earth altogether is an integral part of their common vision. Abandon this earth? Why? Because it is deserted and useless? Abandon it to go where? To other planets or to nothingness? This is a horrible perspective. It creates a terrible impact on the human psyche. The feeling of being forced to be like a refugee: 'We who are escaping'.

Milton is positive in saying, 'Look for the pieces'. When you search in this way for something, you gain knowledge. Milton is saying that the truth came once as a revelation. We still want an ethical system. 'Truth' has not yet been erased from our language, but it is just a matter of time.

Instead of truth we talk about 'discussion', supposedly a process which leads towards objective resolutions. As a matter of fact it leads nowhere. Person-to-person confession leads somewhere. There is a saying: 'When two of us are talking together God is with us. When three of us are talking together everyone is pretending to be God'. We try to get rid of the concept of truth and I am saying, 'Wait a second, this is the wrong process, even if truth is something nostalgic and sentimental which doesn't exist any more, do not kill this sentiment in your psyche, in your being'.

We are told that in postmodernist theory every expression and every action can be presented as purely objective – factually endorsed, even rituals of self-harm, body piercing, masturbation. In this context, my perspective towards truth may seem nostalgic, but my nostalgia is towards an appreciation of nature. Nature teaches itself. It speaks for itself. It is history, myth, legend, fairy tale. So what will you pass on to your children? Are you going to pass on these objective rituals of today? What are you going to teach them? You have to be careful because if you show too many perspectives as in postmodernism, you negate, or at least, neutralize, the concept of truth, putting it in the archive of our active mental life.

Of course, I believe that there is nothing like one fundamental truth, but truth exists somewhere in small pieces. Our life in theatre – indeed, any life – is to make this incredible effort to pick, to search for these small pieces of truth. That's why I make expeditions to indigenous communities, to look for the small pieces of something, the gesture, the word, the saying, the tone, the expressiveness of breathing, the devotion to that and only that place.

Through this identification that you perceive in somebody, through his shameful gesture, her trembling tone of voice, his imperceptible word, her widening eyes disseminating amazement, you build your own model of theatre and it affects your life as well.

There are fragments of behaviour which have happened thousands of times. We recognize them because they have their repetition in the past. This is not nostalgia, it is a fact. You recognize one particular gesture as true because it has a genealogy that has existed for millennia. But those with a postmodernist view, or those looking for a brave new world, call this nostalgia. For me, it is a fact and the only stable reference point. The only one that keeps me in order. If we lose our reference points, we can forget about our lives. We will be like wandering, lost souls.

Healer at the annual
Orthodox celebration,
eastern Poland, 1990.
Photo: Alison Hodge.

Gusła (*Sorcery*) in the Old Arian Chapel, Gardzienice. *Back*: Wanda Wróbel, Krzysztof Czyżewski, Jan Tabaka. *Middle*: Iga Rodowicz, Mariusz Gołaj, Jan Bernad. *Front*: Anna Zubrzycka. *Photo*: Zygmunt Rytka.

Gusła (*Sorcery*) in the Old Arian Chapel, Gardzienice. *Photo*: Zygmunt Rytka.

The disused
Arian chapel –
the studio for
training and
performing
1977–90 (work
area 5m × 7m).
Photo:
Gardzienice
Archive.

theatre and religion

Why is theatre dying? Because theatre forgot about its challenge. Every form of theatre in its beginnings aspired to revelation.

Revelation in the most prosaic sense meant to reveal to the audience, to shake them, to arouse them. In the most mystical way, theatre aspired to revelation like the 'voice from above'. Moses receiving the Ten Commandments was a scene of great theatrical revelation.

In ancient drama there are moments when the Gods appear; they interfere with the action or they decide how to end the action. As in Euripides, when Apollo arrives and decides to finish a never-ending procedure of tragic actions. In the Polish language the word is *objawiać*, meaning both 'to reveal' and 'to resolve something'. It means 'like a thunderbolt'. To shake and to reveal. Should one expect miracles during the performance? Yes. You have to know how to prepare the ingredients, ignite the fire under the crucible, and then the actors can transmute their material into gold.

Revelation in the ancient Greek drama occurred in every entrance. When Agamemnon comes back from the Trojan War it is a revelation. The director should ask: How shall I bring him onto the stage when it is such a revelatory, unbelievable moment? The people have already established a completely new model of life. They don't want Agamemnon to come back from Troy because he would be an intruder. From another perspective he comes from another world, he is not the same Agamemnon. In ancient Greek drama, things change in such a way that nothing is the same in the next act, or even in the next couple of scenes. It is a revelatory change. A metamorphosis.

The word 'miracle' has religious connotations, but in theatre we cannot simply reject all the technology of religion. We cannot give it up, because we are not only cutting out our spirituality but we are neutering ourselves. I did an experiment with the texts from three performances, *Avvakum*, *Carmina Burana* and *Metamorphoses*. I used texts which are full of words strictly directed towards God: 'God', 'Holy Mother', 'Jesus' and 'Holy Spirit'. I erased all these words and the texts were suddenly poetic, sensual, and simply human, dismantled of their doctrine. Erase the words which the times dictate and you have an exclamation from the human heart.

Just refer to St Paul's song of love, commonly known as his first letter to the Corinthians. I am talking about great art. Those words 'God', 'Holy Mother' and so on are just the generators. Sometimes if you erase these words, you will even see a strong contradiction, a criticism, a fight with religion.

Miracle, revelation, metamorphosis

I have a triangle – three key words in my work: metamorphosis, miracle and revelation. They create an equalization that has to be realized in theatre. Which comes first? Revelation. But we live in a deaf world, so the old messages are bypassing us and instead we have an exchange of information. If we decide about our lives solely on the basis of information, it means that there is no place for revelation.

Foyer theatre

The most exciting moment in theatre is before the performance starts, in the theatre foyer, when people come with hope and trust and beliefs which are not yet polluted or disappointed. Of course, the audience does not come to the theatre exclusively for social reasons but this public space is an important part of theatre. If we come just to sit in auditorium chairs, which isolate one person from another, it means theatre and society are dead because it reveals a certain tendency for alienation. Humanity has always been strong and powerful when people unite themselves, and the rituals (which enabled this process) generated human potential. When you are alienated you only think about the ritual of the graveyard. The foyer is the last ritualistic space of being together and of having hope.

Hope is always related to revelation and to miracle. The foyer is like the doctor's waiting room, which creates the same expectation of hope, so here we are close to the value of healing and the meaning of theatre. However, when we talk about the healing aspects of theatre we are dismissed as being similar to those who talk about religion. Healing in the theatre means to make sublime, to focus your mind, to stimulate it. We kill the healing sense of theatre if we ignore the expectation of the theatre-goers.

We should study the foyer, the waiting room. Theatre academics, sociologists and psychologists should go to the foyer and study it as it is, and study the foyer which is inside each of us. Let's study this expecting room and we will see how much theatre is concerned with our expectation of a miracle, the healing process.

'Oficyna' before restoration, 1977. *Photo*: Gardzienice Archive.

'Oficyna' after restoration, 2000. *Photo*: Przemysław Sieraczyński.

Students warming up outside the cottage (Chałupa) in Gardzienice – the first shelter and gathering place. *Photo*: Alison Hodge.

natural phenomena

The rehabilitation of ugliness

In Poland, the authorities, the cultural politicians, created the notion of a 'common culture'. But in this eastern region there was a mixture of many cultures. There was a huge Jewish population of three million people living in the ghettos, where they maintained their Yiddish language. There were a lot of Ukrainian and Belorussian enclaves, villages and societies, very isolated in the sense of being without any other influences. Gypsies were small minorities but very visible, as were Russians because they dominated this east-central part of Poland for 200 years. Then there were cultures like Georgian and Armenian, Byzantine culture, and Lithuanian, which is a separate, exclusive and original culture that has a completely different language. This was the melting pot of Europe.

When I began working in this region, I drew on references from life from these existing, traditional cultures, but also I referred to inspirational writers and painters, works that were in relation to indigenous tradition. I used these works, and through developing my theatre practices I discovered that this is where my roots are.

Let me give you one example. Van Gogh was an inspirational figure for me, with his life and his relationship to existence: to ordinary people, to the landscape, to the clod of earth. He was not creating symbols but allegories. He took a given piece of existence – whether it was a man, a plant, a piece of land – and then presented it in a way that makes us feel that suddenly we're confronted with its essence.

In his picture *Wheatfield with Crows*, he shows the moment of passing through to eternity, the moment of death. Look how the black birds are flying away in this incredible earth storm. In my theatre work, I try to show the realities which represent ordinary, trivial, vulgar existence transformed into allegories of the infinite. You may not know, but I know, how much a flock of crows are trivial, vulgar, ordinary and repugnant. I know because they were around my head for decades. When dozens of them suddenly take off from the trees they were occupying, you see this black cloud and you hear this terrible cawing, and your heart jumps into your mouth. You have evidence of an allegory of fear.

I want to stress how much ugliness is interwoven with beauty. Van Gogh used the term 'the rehabilitation of ugliness', which is very important in my work. This term should be a slogan and exclamation. John Berger talks about a 'theatre of indifference'. He describes people who are somehow very ordinary and yet you can receive through their body language messages which are significant because they are close to the texture of existence: death, suffering, laughter, passion, amazement and so on. Suddenly the ordinary is metamorphosed into the infinite.

I still have a copy of Van Gogh's picture of *Sorrow*, where a supposedly ugly woman is posing with her naked neck and with long, black, untidy hair. Van Gogh's self-portraits are concerned with the rehabilitation of ugliness as well. They are dealing with dissonance, with small drops of truth, which once belonged to one common shape and then shattered, as Milton describes, into pieces.

Rehabilitation means to revalidate. It does not mean to show the surface of these images, which would be immediately rejected, but to show their inner energy, their incredible strength, which speak about the particularity of human beings. Revalidation generates the beauty of character which is other than that modelled by the mass media, whose images are devoid of character. These rehabilitated creatures are beautiful because they are truthful.

Realism and transcendence

'Natural phenomena' is the term I use for ordinary existence. Natural phenomena concerns the human being in nature − something that alarms us, alarms our senses, alarms our perception.

There is a link between natural phenomena and high art. This process of metamorphosing from one to the other is a lost understanding. Euripides was an exponent of this knowledge. Aristophanes famously accused Euripides of mixing prosaic life with the serious arts; of mixing ordinary events with memorized, sanctified myths. But Euripides found a way to build a model through metamorphosing the trivial events of ordinary life into the highest reality. That's why we can say he somehow rehabilitated the ugliness of ordinary life.

I also want to refer to Van Eyck because his work is an example of this remarkable combination of realism and transcendence. In *The Adoration of the Lamb*, his Ghent altarpiece, Van Eyck created realistic, almost naturalistically painted landscapes, interiors, architecture, portraits and images which are in direct reference to his time. He depicts the world in which he was living, but at the same time, through inscribing mythical details and symbols, he suddenly achieves an astounding effect. He switches realism into transcendence. He goes to such extremes that he breaks the border of realism and enters into the other world. Realism touches transcendence. We normally don't bring these ideas together. We see them as complete opposites. Why? I see them as neighbours.

In my performance of *Metamorphoses*, a group of deformed but identifiable peasants exclaim, 'We the family of Plato, we know only that which is holy, spiritual, noble and highest'. This is the famous exclamation taken from Apuleius. I am not making an ironic commentary on a peasant environment. I am saying, that which appears to be so-called primitive is not necessarily empty but can be filled with the highest values. Just look from another corner, watch from another perspective.

Our training is drawn from this realistic inspiration. I pick those moves, turns, curves and dynamics which have the most impact. Then, later on, like a painter, working with the tempo, rhythm, changes in the dynamics, I use the same gesture but try to transform it into an allegorical language which breaks the realism.

The intention is to retain the essential quality of the gesture. The difference between the training itself, and using the training in performance, is that in the performance it belongs to completely another canvas, another composition, and another context. And this context already influences each particular gesture. It doesn't mean that it changes its origins, but it shows it from another perspective and you have the feeling that you are taken to another world.

romanticism

You can recognize that the sources of my work are in Romanticism, but remember that almost half of my work has occurred in a new reality, a semi-democratic system. The context is still very wild but Poland has become very Westernized, otherwise the larger family of Western countries would never take us seriously.

I am the Last Mohican in this defeated situation. The last one, in this wasteland, to try to defend values which are not fitting to reality. I am defending an idea of personal freedom which allows me to choose the subject of my work, which is deeply connected to me, and those similar to me, which is not overthrown by the common need of the society, which is money, sausage, vodka and success.

Some people say, particularly in the West, that Romanticism is a retreat into an internal world. I would say, 'Not at all. You never beat the wall with your head if you are not Romantic. You never dream about journeying to the stars if you are not Romantic. Who are the Romantics? They are the true explorers. You dream and you have an incredible will to touch, to follow your will, risking everything'.

My personal freedom is in opposition to the needs of the so-called society. This semi-democratic society wants me to serve it in the way in which it can imagine culture. I am told, 'Make Gardzienice a beer or vodka dance hall'. I say, 'I will tell you who are Euripides, Electra and Iphigenia. I will tell you something about your mixed heritage because of the bones of the wandering nations that you can find beneath your house. Who are they? What does it mean to be a Pole?' The bones you can dig here are the bones of Ukrainian, Jewish, Scandinavian – Vikings were here, Romans. You can find an echo of many, many nations.

'We are pure Poles! We speak this language and we want our Catholic Church and priests. The priests are telling us who we are and we know who we are, we know our prayers – that's our identity'. I say, 'But that's my freedom. I am defending the right to do what I want with my time, not what you want'. In this abandoned, forgotten land, I want to protect the right to one's own time.

I am protecting the right to educate young people in the way that nature speaks to them. When they come to Gardzienice from the cities, to participate in the Academy for Theatre Practices, they understand and they respect, through their experience here, that the sources of creation are not only in the human mind. They are everywhere in living nature. It is only a question of being able to perceive, to see.

section two | **practice**

chapter 5

expeditions

For many years we started our expeditions[15] when a new piece of work was in progress. This experience constitutes what I call a process of 'naturalization' of the performance. We travelled by foot to the villages and met with the indigenous communities, hearing their songs and stories and their music.

Expeditions embrace both the life of the participants and the creative theatrical process. It is an unusual pre-performative process because we wander through the landscape and the stage is everywhere. The expedition sharpens your awareness and your senses. It opens the channels of absorbing the phenomena of life, not just from other people but also from all that surrounds you. Consequently, when it opens these channels, it inspires.

Imagine a theatre ensemble packing their equipment into a bus and driving far away from the city life to hidden territories where there is no theatre, where the settlements and villages are isolated. Somewhere far in the mountains, for instance, where the roads are poor. The people get out of the bus at a prearranged place and they walk, pushing all their equipment on a loaded cart. They pull this cart and they travel for days and nights with the landscape, the map of Mother Earth as the stage. They stop on the way and they rehearse a scene. They find a stream and create a camp next to it, where they continue the work. They train, practise the music, rehearse the dialogues and the common scenes. There is a director, actors and some observers, who have been invited to participate, and some students.

When the ensemble arrives in the villages, they have to organize themselves as if they were nomads without any preparation. They introduce themselves to the local people. They have to make clear what their journey, their 'pilgrimage', is about, because otherwise they are treated as aliens. As we know, aliens are usually exterminated, because that is the natural reaction of these people who defend their earth from generation to generation.

How do you identify yourself? Through your own song, you announce yourself as someone who is an innocent. Through this 'concert', you present what your sense of life is about, through your work. If you were a carpenter you would offer to do some carpentry; if a shoemaker you would offer to repair some shoes. If you were a trader you would offer some exchange but you are an actor, a singer, a space arranger (because theatre is about adapting, transforming and metamorphosing the space), so this is what you offer. Your task is to demonstrate how you can transform the square of the given settlement into an arena – changing the fire brigade's half-ruined building into a castle, switching the small, local river into the Styx, the border between two realities.

The process of journeying, of 'pilgrimage', is so rich; life and art in this context are so interwoven. So many momenta, so many incidents, casual events, are enriching life and your artistic process, that you can build a huge story on one expedition alone.

The role of the director/gatherer

This sort of journey, which I call expedition, has to have rules. It has to be framed, otherwise the intentions of every participant can pull it in different directions. There has to be one leader. It is not about authoritarianism. It is about accepting extreme responsibility for other human beings. It is more than just a theatre director rehearsing a play five or six hours a day, as in administrative theatre. This is someone who directs life twenty-four hours a day. The art of theatre and cultural activity is a segment in the greater plan of survival.

Our democracies have complexes: any idealistic leadership, which is not administratively accounted for, or publicly elected, is treated as a problem. In this context, the director is regarded as someone who has suspicious ambitions. But in homogenous societies the leader remains in that position as long as she or he proves they have the ability to deal with people's passions, imagination and creativity. Someone who is able to shape, to carve and to tune them. To direct means to make sublime in the chemical sense: to transform from one state to another. Metaphorically, it means to 'make poetic'.

The expedition director has to interfere with poetic delicacy, with diplomacy and with knowledge about human beings. He or she has to know when to wake up at the proper time in order to train, to rehearse at the correct moment, to arrange a breakfast, which is already a rehearsal, because the table can create the possibility of uniting the ensemble to work on songs or text. It is the responsibility of the director to switch the prosaic process of eating into a ceremonial, artistic situation.

The expedition is a natural process, which can test the director's skill, talent, generosity and subtlety. You have to deal with difficult life situations and you can only do this properly when your creative process has gone through these difficulties. Imagine a situation when the whole village is against you and you have to win them over. You must immediately direct the musical and theatrical event that will say who you are, what your humanity is about, why you are there at all, but also you have to prove your usefulness. (Village people are practical and they want to know if you are useful or not.) So, if as a director you find that at a certain moment the only way to be accepted is for the actors to offer to help in the fields, you do so.

Reconnaissance

In my model of expeditions, 'reconnaissance' precedes the arrival of the ensemble. I send someone who has a high level of communication and empathy to walk the terrain and draw a map of the 20-kilometre (12-mile) stage through which the group will travel.

This person points out the places of particular significance: those with geographical power, beauty and physical challenge. He or she identifies where stops can be made and where there are places which can 'generate' the rehearsals, because there are certain places which can influence and inspire rehearsals. The expedition contains the mythologies of wandering people and the possible behaviour inside us that our grandparents, for example, encountered. Once we start the journey, we find the generations are talking through us. So the geographical reconnaissance recognizes the map of the terrain through which we will walk and identifies the settlements to which we 'alien people' will come.

The reconnaissance team of one to three people reports back very precisely, as if to a prosecutor, about what they have found. How difficult was the route? What was the wind like? What were the natural sounds in the landscape? How thick was the forest? Are there any sheltered places? What is the settlement like sociologically? How many buildings? Where is the central square? What are the main buildings? Who are the people? And, most importantly, who is the one we are looking for, the one who is the culture of the village? My cultural religion does not understand culture as a statistic but that which is contained and preserved in one particular human being, or in one family. So, who is the Homer of the given settlement?

The person who is the culture

The person who is the culture of the village is usually the artist or the so-called artist: an animator or activist, described anthropologically as a trickster, or magician or shaman. In Latin this is the *stultus dei*, meaning 'God's fool'. In Polish we say 'głupiec Boży'. The one who is respected by part of the village for their unusual deeds, or useless travel where they made no money, lost their jacket, but came back with a lot of experiences and stories. Some people in the village are happy with them but a larger part of the village think that this person is an idiot because they don't have any way of dealing with them, and they don't have any wealth. They are frequently artists or musicians who often don't have a high social level and are not respected by the village, but are very useful because every time local festivities take place they are called to play and to sing. If you arrange a festive situation around them all the village people will come.

A person on reconnaissance has to find such people, and I call them 'our people living amongst aliens'; we say 'he is our soul'. We are able to communicate with these people. For some reason, they immediately respond to us, even risking their relationships within the community, if there is not a generally welcome response from the village.

The expectation of the 'so-called artist' is archetypical. In a homogenous society there is always someone who expects aliens. They believe that one day some people will come from far away, from across the oceans, those people spoken about in the old stories. It is a typical situation in every society and every group, so it is symbolic. The person always expects that these strangers will identify the 'so-called artist' as some sort of VIP and will transform their life. Maybe the strangers will offer a contract or possibilities to travel, but even if they just communicate and explain existence in a different way they already transform the life of the one who is waiting.

❖ A gathering in the Carpathian Mountains

(Excerpt from the commentary to a film by Tony Hill for the Royal Shakespeare Company, made on expedition in the Ukraine, 1991)

Last night we brought people from all over this region together. One local singer, a group of musicians from Zamagoria, a group of young women singers from a nearby village and a storyteller from the other side of the mountains. It was a complicated operation to bring them all together for an evening, and to establish a situation in which all of them would be able to collaborate and to create the right conditions in which theatre would appear.

And yet it happened. Last night you could see how the people came together perfectly in the space. They have an instinctive knowledge, which doesn't demand any direction or instruction about how to re-create their world, because 'gathering' is fundamentally connected to their tradition, their nature and their culture.

There were young women in one corner, singers in another and a musician standing against a wall – beautifully composed – like an icon. The way that the children were sitting together with arms around each other, watching, was like an image from Brueghel. Then there were outsiders hanging around the main doors waiting for something, probably for quarrels, fights, controversies and maybe some alcohol. One after another entrances were made into this room, which was already packed with people. Finally, the main actor came. It was an incredible moment: everything was already boiling – there was music playing, there had been presentations of local instruments, a lot of dancing.

Suddenly, the doors opened and the people who were blocking the doorway parted. A young girl through this corridor of people led a very old, seemingly blind man with his violin. There was total silence. We brought him to the front of the stage where the main musicians were sitting. The stage setting was prepared for him. Immediately all the elders came and surrounded him, while others whispered about him.

Who is this man? He is the legend of this terrain. He is the culture of this terrain. This man is the biggest symbol of this region. He is eighty years old, his name is Mogur, he is a violin player and he has created a lot of music which has been played in this area. His life was very difficult, he lived through all the catastrophes that so powerfully infected this region – and he survived. And legend has it that he survived thanks to his music. He is a self-educated musician – every piece of music, which he composed, comes from his dreams. When you say the name Mogur in this area of the Carpathians, people are immediately more attentive. I didn't believe that he would come to the gathering because we have tried so many times before to reach him and to work with him. He was like a vanishing point – somewhere and everywhere like a myth, like a legend. So we succeeded in bringing a living legend to this gathering. ❖

Rules

The rules of the expedition include the following:

1   To make a journey that starts, lasts for four or five days, and ends.
2   It has to have proper dramaturgy.
3   No alcohol is drunk except ceremonially in order not to break the traditions.
4   You do not look for material advantages. Material goods are not bought in such a way that it seems as though your intention is to gain people's property.
5   You must not undermine the process of journeying for personal reasons. For example, a performance has finished at midnight and the gathering that followed, instead of lasting two hours, lasts four. The plan is to complete another sequence of the road through part of the night. The strength and power of this sequence of the road is unusual, and this is the only occasion to experience the influence of the environment in a way that inspires your artistic imagination. You

cannot refuse because of fatigue. You must do it except when it is evident that people physically are unable to manage it.

6   You must agree to do all the necessary physical work, which will create a safe existence for everyone. You have to build a camp, cook, pull the cart.

7   If the director says to an actor that they will be the best communicator with the people in the given village, you must not reject this task. You are being given a role. You are the text and are going to persuade the village people as you would the audience on stage. As an actor, you check your abilities, your means of expression. This role has to be carefully allocated; the director's sensibility, his way of reading the actor's potential, is important.

8   You are obliged to be clean and leave every domestic place in order. If you are looked after in somebody's house, you have to know that it demands your gratitude and that you know how not to interfere with their domestic life. You bring joy, energy, helping hands. You never use your hosts, although you allow yourself to be used.

9   The day is scheduled so that there is always time for training, several times at different times in the day or night. It is obligatory. Sometimes it is used just to wake up, sometimes as part of the rehearsal process.

Incidents

There are any number of incidents that happen on expeditions, and I insist that the actors retain them. The actor's task is to memorize them and to have an album of the never-ending phenomena, which show you, the human being, in different contexts and shapes and under different circumstances suspended between earth and heaven. You not only see people all around you as if from Brueghel, but also from Chagall, from Bosch, Malczewski and Wyspiański. You not only see pictures which reflect this particular geographical region, but those which are much more universal, which can be found in other continents. Life is not reality, which diminishes the arts – life is a magic reality which enriches the arts. It is simply a question of the ability of your fantasy to identify and transform it into an artistic opus.

❖ Identify and transform

(From a speech made at the 5th Performance Studies Conference, Aberystwyth in April 1999)

Myths are stories about times when people, animals and plants were not separated from each other but were aspects of a living whole. When neither thought was separated from emotions, nor gesture from word, nor philosophy from music. Nowadays we are taught that our education is connected almost entirely to the verbal tradition. It is difficult to question this, but in fact we must do so because we know that through this form of learning we feel impoverished, incomplete, 'uncompleted'.

Mythical thinking moulds natural reality. It combines various elements of the natural world in order to build a new model with an inner unity and logic. For us Europeans there were two familiar cultures founded on myth: the ancient Greek and the indigenous, so-called 'primitive' world.

It is impossible to explain myth; you can only identify with it and then eventually express this identification. Words are weak in the face of myth because their domain is to explain, whereas myth asks us to embody, to 'ensoul', to inspirit, to enchant.

Mikhail Bakhtin recommended a philosophical, artistic, intuitive way of exploring the deep structures of culture in opposition to a purely rational approach. I understand his recommendation as **Identify and transform**.

Euripides dealt with myths. Can we assume that, through collecting fragments, Bakhtin's 'superior sequences', from different elements of the natural world, Euripides was thinking mythically? **Identify and transform**. He combined different elements of the reality he experienced within a given mythology in order to build a model with an inner logic and unity which embodies, 'ensouls', inspirits and enchants the chosen myth.

It is important to remember that Euripides was a composer. Paradoxically, this is a public secret. For centuries after his death people sang the musical parts of his dramas and couplets while his plays were not performed. The parallel between myth and music is obvious. Mythical structures prefigure musical forms. When the contents of myth are suppressed within the unconscious, only music can retrieve the thought of myth. Myth is not articulated through thought, word or image, but through sound.

The ancient Greek form of education was called *paideia*. The word means 'to cultivate, to grow, to breed'. Music and movement were not regarded as additional to the word. They were an integral part of education. These forms were not taught for a social purpose but in order to search for the truth and sense of existence. In Lucian's[16] treatise on dance, he stresses that the purpose of movement and gesture was to be able to connect with their mythical contents.

Paideia was a consciously pursued ideal, referring to the way in which the human being is cultivated. It can be taken as a complete theatre with all its attributes. When in an indigenous village I see a grandfather teaching his grandson a song, gesturing the words and sounds and stamping the syllables, I think of *paideia*. A complex theatre. The grandfather inscribes, his grandson reads the line of life of music, the line of life of the body and the word. In mythical structures one means of expression enlightens the other. Word enlightens movement, movement enlightens music, music enlightens word. Each explains the other. They are intertwined like a wreath, like motifs within a fugue.

The myths talk to each other throughout the centuries. The sounds speak to each other throughout the centuries. Myth can be articulated through sound because sound is a chromosome of myth and consequently contains the chromosome codes of culture. Through the sounds of existing indigenous cultures we are able to retrieve the sounds of ancient culture, come closer to ancient myth.

In *The Golden Ass*, Apuleius deals with the myth of transformation. Lucius, the hero, searches for himself. He is transformed into an ass and makes his journey through life. He finds himself when he identifies with myth. The words describe his passionate journey but we also have a remnant of sound from history which survived in indigenous culture: the calling 'Hee haw!' which expresses the suffering of the search for ourselves and the glory of being found. Hee haw! **Identify and transform**!

Until the Renaissance, a popular ritual took place in churches. A live donkey was led into the 'temple' and, instead of the sacramental 'Amen', the priests and congregation were calling, 'Hee haw!' Instead of 'So be it', the Dionysian 'Here I am'.

Didactics should be concerned with the search for ourselves and not the imposition of verbal structures. Theatre is probably the only field of human activity that can be paideic. A theatre from the spirit of sounds.

Apollo skinned Marsyas after he defeated him in a musical competition. Marsyas was a Silenus from Phrygia, the motherland of Dionysus. The satyr brothers of Marsyas were brothers of Dionysus, a traveller who drinks wine, sings, dances and cries. He introduces us into the mysteries of metamorphosis. He helps us to identify. Apollo instructs, Dionysus opens the eyes. ❖

On expedition, northeast Poland, 1989. *Photo*: Gardzienice Archive.

Crossing the Bug River, eastern border, Poland, 1978. *Photo*: Gardzienice Archive.

On expedition, eastern border, Poland, 1978. *Photo*: Gardzienice Archive.

'No Trespassing' – on expedition in northeast Poland, 1981. *Photo*: Gardzienice Archive.

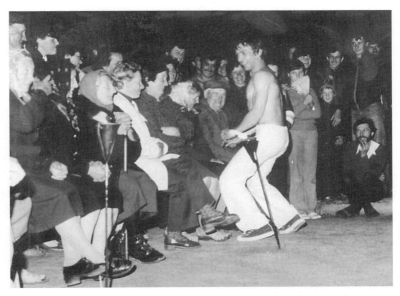

Jan Tabaka in a transitional moment from *Evening Performance* to *Gathering*, 1980. *Photo*: Gardzienice Archive.

A gathering in eastern Poland, 1980. *Photo*: Gardzienice Archive.

gatherings

I am of the opinion that 'gathering'[17] is a moment of theatre born of itself. The traditional gathering has, within it, the fundamental structure and principles of drama. It has enormous theatricality and dynamism. If you observe the traditional gatherings in the villages where the people meet to sing, play their music and tell their stories, you will see that they are richer and more developed than many dramas done on the stage. My theatre work has been an attempt to try and deal with this.

The performance and gathering

Once you have arrived in a village, the preparations for the performance and the gathering are done in a very visible way to engage as large a proportion of the community as possible, such as building a common stage. Small groups of actors walk from house to house. They do small performances in front of, or inside, the houses. They are somehow identifying themselves and announcing what they are inviting people to participate in. You may rehearse with local musicians, and if there are storytellers you try to include them as well, if not in the performance scenario, then in the gathering. So the preparations should animate the local community as much as possible.

Through the residence in the village a lot happens. Situations can be very disturbing but also inspiring and energizing for the actors. The director has to be able to respond to the incidents – to include them and to absorb them into the structure of the performance or gathering. In a well-functioning environment, once you pluck the string, all the instruments play and people come with surprising offerings. Not only do they want to help you with food but also with offers of support: to build the stage by themselves, to accompany the ensemble in the next stage of wandering and to insist that the next village properly welcomes you and treats you in an appropriate way.

Such an intervention into the body of a given society demands a high level of seriousness in the presentation of your skills. You must demonstrate your own abilities as perfectly as possible. If you do not ignore, you will not be ignored. If you present your skills, they will respond with their highest abilities. You do not treat these people as primitive, uneducated or culturally underdeveloped. You treat them more seriously than the audiences in professional theatres. It is so obvious to say this in terms of guaranteeing a serious response, but it also enables you to create and improve the ethics of your own work. You teach yourself that your standards cannot drop just because you are in a place where there are no critics, no tickets and where the applause will not necessarily be loud, and where the resonance of your work will not bring you typical public advantages. You are doing your work on the highest possible level.

The competitive aspect strongly resonates in these societies and this creates a high level of skill. They wish to raise themselves to a higher performance level in the same way that you, as the visitors, are trying to do. If you present a higher quality in the next song – say, moving from solo to harmony – the local people look for an appropriate musical response to show their skill. It is not a competition but it is to 'rise up', like a flourishing process in which you see the energy of beauty, of effort, of searching for the next revelation. This is the ideal. The ability of the animators to encourage this is a very important aspect of 'gathering'. If you don't have this quality to encourage, to dynamize, to open the other side, you do not create this elevatory process. Instead it becomes fixed on a certain level of consequent exchange – first you sing, then they sing, and so on. The dramaturgy is not fermenting.

Our intention is not just to bring a performance to a village. We present fragments of our performance as we are working on it, but the main point is to stimulate a gathering. The real performance and the real event is the gathering.

The performance demonstration is very important because it allows you to identify your work. The village is never passive during the performance because this sort of society still has a liveliness, an immediate reaction to an action, a picture, to events, happenings. But the gathering is much more significant because you are changing the passive audience into an active one.

The expedition tests and proves the strength and the 'causing effect' of the performance, of the scenes, of acting, of timing – all the aspects which indicate whether it is alive or not. It is a very good training camp for learning your craft.

I don't want to work with an actor who is a stage animal that can do whatever the director explains to him. I want to work with an actor with whom I can talk about the phenomena of life, of nature. We can respond together, because we share our experiences and our openness to the phenomena, widening our fields of perception. The best actor is a sort of hooligan because the hooligan has strong sensibilities, is perceptive and is able to re-create. It is something to do with their adaptability, of being able to transform themselves in the situation and to transform the given situation. It is like being a trickster and magician simultaneously. So they can do tiny deeds which cause bigger effects.

The actors I work with are not the sort who, in an everyday situation, appear as personalities. The personality actor is immediately understood as being there in order to be celebrated. Those actors are not celebrating the village people, nor are they celebrating with them. That's another world. We are Argonauts, not invaders. We are not conquistadors; rather, we ask if we can share with them the water from their village well.

Naturalization

We could arrange a discussion with the audience after the gathering, but once people start to discuss what they have seen they engage with their experience on a completely different level. This is interpretation.

When the gathering event happens, the symphony of active reactions and dialogue is instructive and sharpens the quality of the 'acts'. It immediately stimulates and alchemizes the actors because it is voice to voice, body against body, move against move, word against word. The actor can tell whether he is capturing the attention of the audience and whether he possesses all their senses. At the same time, the actor is challenged to tune his way of acting to the different levels of this symphony of reactions in order to tune the audience. This is an effective school for actors, helping them to naturalize their means of expression. It is similar to a Pansori opera singer whose voice has been cultivated in a classroom and on the stage of the opera house. Then they go to the waterfalls to test the strength, quality and the colour of the voice, exercising it against the noise of the water. It is the same process of naturalization for the actor dealing with this rebel audience, who are not told to sit, be silent, to be attentive for several hours, which always induces boredom. In contemporary theatre the audience is administrated very, very much.

When Isadora Duncan danced in front of Russian workers during the Revolution, on an improvised stage in a factory, we have been told that she had a phenomenal spiritual impact. She was tuning herself and the audience. Her art was naturalized through this confrontation.

I play a certain theatre composition 'towards' these people. I try to see, through their expressive way of communicating, whether the form of the composition is with inner energy and has all the necessary structural values, tempo, dynamics, the appropriate impact which captures the audience. Is the form forming them, unifying them as a common eye and heart? Or is it just dispersing them into many beings? If it doesn't work I deconstruct it, rebuild it and try again.

There are many aspects to the naturalization process. The first concerns the actor testing and sharpening his means of expression. The second is the opportunity provided for the director to test the composition. The third is the 'live interferences' from the audience/ participants. Those reactions which we call 'dialogue' can be incorporated into the structure of the work in progress. I call these 'incidents'. For example, in Gusła[18] we played in a fire-brigade barn. There was a chorus led by Mariusz Gołaj[19] singing songs and creating a lively parade. Suddenly, one person jumped into the chorus and started to lead with his own half-drunk way: the step, the waving, the way the shoulders are held and how the head is swaying. This was a mixture of vulgar, everyday, prosaic behaviour, which can be transformed, mainly through the music and dance, in order to reach a higher aesthetic level. I learnt a lesson in understanding how art mixes so-called 'vulgar reality' with so-called 'higher reality'.

The fourth aspect of the naturalization process is the search for texts, which are the result of this 'interference in dialogue'. For example, an actor speaks a monologue and a voice from the crowd is constantly adding something. Immediately it is a dithyrambic situation with a solo actor in relation to the choir, but in this moment the real choir is the audience. Part of the naturalization process is the inclusion of these interferences, but also interjections from the audience. This is when they intervene with material belonging to their own lives. Through them your text can be refreshed because the content of their interjection can influence the content of your work in progress.

When we were doing expeditions with *Forefather's Eve*,[20] we were simply rhythmicizing a poetic text and the people would answer with their own song. They found that the way of 'waving' with the text was to find something which was similar in song. In one incident, they showed me that Mickiewicz's exclamative poem is in relation to a song which they had instinctively recalled. Another village may sing another song in response. It doesn't matter. It means that the poem evokes a response and my task is to choose which of these songs is most appropriate to incorporate as an interlude into the performance.

The text is also the body. While the actor performs an action, some-one is trying to get into dialogue by mimicking, rejecting, playing with it. You get an Artaudian 'double'. You cannot ignore it, you have to absorb it later on in the rehearsal process – even by putting the double on stage, because the double is like a mirror which amplifies the strength of the acting.

The actor must not ignore these responses. If you do, you become a defensive actor, just working with your set pattern. But performance, in the process of naturalization, is fermented in a positive way only if you never ignore but constantly respond. The actor can suspend a response if, for example, there is violence, but he has to get into dialogue with this performance, which is now happening in the audience. Such interventions determine the energy of the performance.

Energy has to be injected into the theatre. It is the most dramatic and immediate problem today. Energy is leaking out of theatre. That's why, as with any living organism which is losing energy, theatre is decomposing. That's why this process of naturalization is so important. I can say this because it has been proved through the expeditions and gatherings. The reason why people get together for ceremonies and festive occasions is a matter of energy. That's how theatre was reborn in ancient Greece: the Dionysian mysteries were very much concerned with energy, rebirth.

The fifth aspect of naturalization is concerned with the chalice into which you pour wine – the space. Maybe theatre is decomposing because all the magic is supposedly contained in the theatre buildings but, as we know, magic can only happen in particular places. That's why ritual spaces in the past were carefully chosen – holy places. On expedition, village people will not necessarily come to an arbitrary place for a gathering. Common places demand an administrative way of behaving. If we go to church, we behave according to the demands of the space; the same with a school, and so on. It is necessary to install the event in a place which on the one hand has a large margin for self-freedom, and on the other hand a talkative space which speaks itself – a space which is impressive aesthetically, filled with its own content and vibrations. Ancient people chose those places with a certain wisdom. They were places with a combination of openings to different natural phenomena and immediately gave people a sense of community.

The properly chosen space is a performance itself. Often, the space can be outside the village. Every community has spaces with their own mythology. If you can install yourself there, then people feel enchanted because you reveal the strength and beauty of their space. At the same time, you can play with it.

When we were working on *Avvakum* we went to the Łemko region.[21] One day we came to the Regietow church. A tiny chapel on a crossroads. It looked like a private house. It was beautifully positioned at the edge of the village. There was a river down below with a forest behind it. Perfect geomancy.

We attended the service and the packed space inside played with the outdoor space in such a way that it united the microcosm with the macrocosm. The ceremony involves walking round the outside of the building and coming back inside. This event determined the way of collecting the audience in the space for *Avvakum*. The acting area was a very small packed environment, which was suddenly expanded because the doors within the performance space were broken open, and the actors left and returned through them. In this way I tried to re-create this relationship to outdoor space.

On another expedition in the Łemko territory, we went to an abandoned wooden church in the mountains. It was the only building left in the village after the Poles expelled the Łemko people in 1947. There we rehearsed *Avvakum* in the manner in which the ceremony took place in Regietow. We brought to the church families that had been previously living in this village and we played inside and outside. That was how *Avvakum* was naturalized. The space determined the staging, the audience's position, even the way of acting. When you walk with your work in progress, trying it out in different places, the space co-designs the performance.

❖ On gathering

(From an essay entitled 'Gathering' by W. Staniewski, 1985 – extracts published by The Centre for Performance Research in 1989)

- I was once very taken by what is contained in the root of the notion of 'theatre'. Strangely enough, it has somehow been completely forgotten that the root of the word itself is full of meaning. Theatre is *thea*, which is the definition of a certain state – the act of 'seeing'. 'Seeing through', 'seeing transversely', 'perceiving'. Today, when I talk to you about theatre I think of 'gathering', a theatrical practice which stands above the kinds of theatrical forms cultivated today. It calls together a certain number of people to a chosen place so that, in that place, they can reveal, 'give from themselves', the truth of the cultural and human existence of their society.
- 'Gathering' is not only a form of communicating, but also an 'awakening' of the cultural undercurrents of a given social enclave.
- 'Gathering' stands at the dawn of each cultural tradition. Its various forms were known to every culture. It constituted social relationships, and evaluated all the cultural elements of a given society. 'Gathering' was the solar plexus of society's culture – for example, the *ting* in Norwegian sagas. In Old Norse the word *ting* contains the concept of creation and being.

- Also, in Old English *ting* can mean 'that which is done' or 'is being done'. It means 'action', 'act', 'deeds', 'events', 'appearing' or 'occurrence', 'incident', 'circumstance', 'experience'. All these nuances of the word are necessary in order to explain my understanding of the idea of 'theatre-gathering'. ('Drama' comes from *dromenon* in Greek – a thing which is being done.)

- In local dialects, and in the old Polish language, words such as *gromada* and *zgromadność* mean 'gathering' and *zgromadziciel* refers to the one who gathers, the protagonist; the one who leads a non-stop dialogue, creating a continuous process. The *zgromadziciel* (the 'gatherer') is a conductor, an instigator, a master of ceremonies, a sort of director of the gathering. But this figure is also the one who reveals.

- I define 'gathering' as a discipline of the art of theatre. Therefore it is a certain branch of theatre. The rules of 'gathering' have been decided upon in time immemorial. We reassimilate and practise them.

- 'Gathering' is a social form, which is truly cultivated in native culture. In these indigenous communities 'gathering' is practised as in former times. It is ahistorical and, because of this suspension of time, the people's gestures are ahistorical. These are the gestures which are the signs of real creativity.

- 'Gathering' is a unity – a unity of what is known with what is unknown, what is simple with what is sophisticated. In the 'gathering' opposites are united – the ground of old age with that of youth.

- The nerve point of 'gatherings' are songs. Songs are the source of movement, the source of gestures. The source of rhythm, the source of actions (facts), which are born in that place. Songs are 'done' and 'doing', songs are one of the sources of ahistorical gestures. We know and can attain that they are the source of creation.

- In traditional gatherings, which take place in the homogenous community, there are all the fundamental elements of classical dramaturgy. Wyspiański's *The Wedding* is a poetic transfiguration of 'gathering'. The flesh of the 'gathering' consists of a countless number of colourful incidents which have unequalled theatricality, using all the possible means of expression.

- 'Gathering' encapsulates a different world where values are uncommon. The fate of individual people, the re-ordering of values, less familiar words, uncommon wisdom, different oracles, are vividly expressed.

- 'Gathering' has nothing to do with an anthropological understanding of ritual. It is an unequalled model. It contains the tree of knowledge for theatre. It is not to be mimicked on stage but it is possible to take valuable patterns from it. The experience of 'gathering' offers the practitioner the best education in theatre.

•   In this context, the non-pragmatic gestures of man have changed into a need. From the necessity of repeating these gestures, they have become codified. This significant gestural process is situated in 'gathering'; regardless of the primary reasons which brought human beings together. 'Gathering' is proto-theatre. ❖

section three | technique

chapter 7

musicality

I would like to talk about *musica vitae* or musicality.[22] Music, as it is sometimes understood, is an aesthetic term, having historical connotations. It is related to a codified system operating in terms of notation. Musicality, on the other hand, is for me very close to the spirit. Musicality exists everywhere. I believe that the earth itself is musical.

I believe in instinct and intuition. Soon we will forget them. We will forget that they are part of our nature. We already find for them sophisticated terms such as 'para-natural' and 'para-psychical', and by alienating them from our human nature we cut the umbilical cord, which holds us to our origins. I believe that instinct and intuition are real and I also believe that they cannot exist without musicality. So I am utterly convinced that the earth is musical, that it has musicality and that every part of nature can be musical.

The earth is musical and man is musical. Man can be put out of tune and the same can happen to the earth. Harmony can be restored. But when the strings of man's musicality break, he dies. And when the strings of the earth's musicality break, the earth dies.[23]

The entire world is filled with sound. But natural sounds represent a rich world of music. In the dogs barking in the village and birds singing at my window, I hear musical compositions which inspire me. In so-called tribal music, you can also hear these natural sounds.

Music is a codified system, which contains, limits and tempers the world of sounds. Through it your way of absorbing and responding is conditioned and orientated. That's why our Western music, codified since the Middle Ages, is sometimes referred to as 'reduced'.

The church's influence on Western music is a well-known story. Dissonance was regarded as sin. Ornamentation is not only an expression of emotion but also an intellectual statement – the church found it too dangerous and reduced it. Early Christian civilization did the same with ancient Greek culture. It is a reoccurring pattern which proves our tendency towards reduction. Why? Because reduction is the only way to keep our boiling reality in order.

Everything which sounds beyond the 'edges' of the codified system is musicality. This is as valuable a source of inspiration for theatre work as music itself. Sometimes even more because, as we say, 'music is a key which opens the heart and soul' and musicality is a better key. This is because music represents a certain level of abstraction, whereas musicality can be immediately identified as something that sits inside of me, or something that I hear in real life. Musicality is me. Music, as with any abstract product, loses its relationship with its evoker, its author, and its source. Musicality exists only if it is in permanent connection with its source.

Musicality speaks about identity, it identifies, it says who I am and what I am doing here. It has a direct relationship to existential identity.

There is a pack of dogs that follows our actor, Grzegorz, around the village.[24] One night I was very alarmed by the sound of the dogs. I asked the old man who works here what happened. He told me they had chased a hare. What were they expressing? They expressed themselves in an indispensable moment of life: their state of being. Is this musicality? Of course it is. How can barking dogs be musical? Some might say, 'It is only because your mind and imagination are musical and you can adapt and transform these sounds'. Yes, but it is the source which is connected with its product, and if this wasn't the case I wouldn't be able to transform it.

I would like to have these dogs in my play about Euripides who, as legend tells us, was torn to pieces by dogs at the end of his life. If I could incorporate the music of these animals in their excitement, I would probably find an incredible moment on stage. In acting we must ask whether there are those noises inside of us, which express the same deep nostalgia, possession and other states of mind, and emotion that would be similar to the sound of these dogs.

The actor's expression has been reduced in sound, in the same manner as codified music. I want to expand the actor's *instrumentarium* towards musicality, not only shouts and cries but also all the phenomena, which are sitting inside of us. We can find this musicality in the ritual of lamentation.

My performances incorporate music and musicality. You have to form your artistic proposal and frame it. Once you repeat this framed work, you are developing a uniform structure of sound. Musicality is like a rough diamond, which is properly framed by the gold of the codified music. In the final product, you have to alchemically combine these two things to prove that musicality is in relation to music. It is neither a fantasy nor belonging to another sphere, and it is communicative to human beings.

Codified music can be taken as a well-constructed argument whereas musicality is a 'flow of life'. It is just nature speaking about itself. We don't like to hear this because it is very often overwhelming, like naturalism in the worst sense. That's why it has to be given in the right dosage, so you frame and contextualize the sound.

My practice is concerned with one general principle: the importance of musicality. My aim is to salvage musicality for theatre work. It allows us to widen our perception so that we can experience more than just the usual patterns: the codified music and well-constructed arguments.

Why is this important? We have to do something with the training of our senses, our memory, so that musicality can still be part of our way of communicating with the world, and with 'holiness'. There are three aspects to my process: one is concerned with the expansion of our system of perception; the second with how to find ways to absorb and introduce musicality into our practice; and the third with how to frame it within a performance.

We learn to deal with musicality through our vocal training, which is based on a vast range of musical phenomena – from breathing to lamentation. Lamentation is a clear, practical example of a moment when music and musicality meet together, where a well-constructed argument meets life itself. Bringing musicality into the theatrical structure is a difficult process. It is too easy to overflow the performance with an ocean of different impressions and effects which have come from musicality.

You have to take the most representative pieces and incorporate them into the musical structure.

In *Metamorphoses*, the performance sequence based on Psyche's hysteria, performed by Mariana Sadowska, is a very personal way of expressing an emotional borderline situation for a woman.[25] It involves personal sounds from the actor's inner life, and at the same time this is combined with shouts that turn to laughter, possession, cries, short exclamations. The repertoire of sounds the actor creates comes from her personal body traditions – for instance, from hearing her mother crying, her family quarrelling or her neighbour in a state of despair. These may be some of her reference points but all this musicality has to be framed. In the performance, it is a series of vignettes of sound within a stream, which reflects a certain melody. The actress composes this during a process of 'sounding' in which we also search for the causing effect of the sound. Through identifying the 'causing effects' the actress is kept in balance because such an overflow of life sounds can easily destabilize her emotionally or psychically. You can compare this form to lamentation, which is structured to prevent the women from losing control, from going mad. This overflow of life can tear apart your civilized state of being.

In *Avvakum* we used polyphony, a framed musical style which exists in the Orthodox tradition. It symbolizes heaven; an ideal world, a paradise lost. But heaven is not the zone or space which teaches us about ourselves. Human nature is full of tears, pain and also passionate joy, which disrupt any stability. I asked the actors to look for those sounds in their hidden emotions. And they appeared suddenly, like thunder, breaking through this beautiful polyphony and harmony of orthodox music.

The sounds came from the actor's personal experience but they were also inspired by ceremonial ritualistic ways of sounding. For example, there is the tradition of lamentation, which is related to this technique of 'giving voice'. I explored it for years, finding where this tradition exists in ceremonies, not as an immediate reaction but as part of a ritual. In the springtime, Russian Orthodox women go to the graveyards with food, which they leave for their ancestors' souls, and they sing laments. These are an expression of their emotions, which purify them through this process of 'acting out'. It is a way of shouting their nostalgia, their pain, sadness, loneliness. 'Why did you leave me alone my father or my mother? My husband or my daughter?' This form of lamentation is incorporated into one of the first scenes of *Avvakum*.

Song

Song is a being; it is not just a composition or melody which must simply be sung. Nor is it a pretext for an actor to express his or her ability as an actor. Song is not illustration; it is not only words and melody. In popular song there is a basic distinction between those based on melodies, as in musicals, and those which are based on words, like the protest song. Occasionally, it is a combination of the two. That is not the issue in my work. When I speak about the 'line of life of a song', I am referring to its inner contents, which we have to discover. Song is a hidden territory itself, it is inhabited by a lot of lives. It is like a well-structured metaphor, which can be read in many ways.

I take only those songs that are strongly connected to a given people, or a given tradition. We put aside the melody and the words because, initially, we are trying to find out what is within the deep structure of the song. You get a sort of thicket in which there are certain plants and you try to find out what they represent. You have to penetrate the song through experimentation; through making different combinations of voices and harmonies. You explore different musical ideas, which will suddenly show you different plants within the organism of the song.

I am an idealist. I always believe that there must be a final desti-nation within a song, a way of singing it which explains everything, bringing a sort of catharsis. It is like the search for the Holy Grail: while you are journeying you find different worlds that bring new revelations. The song is an odyssey and you can be misled, you try to prove that a particular harmony synthesized with the particular colours of the voices is correct. But if you continue to penetrate you go further and ev-entually you will probably reach your 'Ithaca'. At that point you are able to make your final decision. I have been working for a long time on one song, *Katolophyromai* (*I Grieve* or *I Cry*), which is one of the relics from Euripides' plays. Suddenly, in rehearsal, after five years, I found the proper understanding and content of that song: 'I cry' means 'I am unleashed'.

Of course, the context in which a song is sung is an important consideration. The professional lamenting women in the Hutsul region stimulated their lamentation in order to get money. They knew when they should lament more desperately and when not. Their deep knowledge of an environment filled with people might be comparable to the appreciation of the professional musician of the acoustic quality in a concert hall. Of course, an environment filled by human beings, in a particular social context, is much more difficult to deal with.

The freedom which musicality gives allows the women to depart from the content of the ritual. A funeral lamentation may begin as a highly structured expression of grief but then the women start to laugh. It is a very far departure towards musicality. They have an ability to incorporate musicality without destroying the reason for their lamentation.

I have a crucial example in my work in *Avvakum*. It was brought from the Polesia region and recorded by Mariana Sadowska from the grave-yards that lamenting Orthodox women visit to share food with their ancestors. The song is a kind of confession through which they try to find answers from the dead. They curse life and the world. They complain that in the difficult moments of life that they have been abandoned – 'You are gone, not with me!' – and they express their hope that the ancestors will help them. This is a traditional lament, which goes on for some time. Suddenly, they switch to their own thoughts, which are connected with practicalities, and they express them unconsciously, as part of the structure, 'Oh God, I didn't pick up the eggs from the chicken today, I have to finish soon.' Then they return to the lamen-tation. Suddenly, one singer turns to another woman, who is 10 metres (33 feet) away, lamenting on another grave, and calls 'Did you hear about such and such a neighbour who was sleeping with so and so!' Then she returns to her lament. This is the flow of musicality with all its consequences. The digression is not only in sound but also content, another story is told, but still within the chalice of the main structure of lamentation which absorbs these departures. This is the 'line of life' of the song.

When I work in the theatre with a complex subject like hysteria, the expressive boundaries are agreed with the actor. The actor may decide about the emotional peripheries, and then, if I want to expand them, I have to prove why this is necessary and it has to be properly controlled. You cannot just push an actor. The peripheries are the limits of expression and thought. Beyond these limits may be a taboo area. The work on hysteria involved the personal experience of the actor but also referred directly to the story of *Amor and Psyche*. As the director, my task was to keep the work within this map of reference points. The song is a container for all this work: the behaviour, the sounds and the musicality. Through the song, it is possible to suggest another world.

Musicality training

The basic musical ideas I would teach an actor are as follows:

Inner musicality

Learn to penetrate the musicality inside oneself. Some aspects are easy to 'pull out of the water'; others are more hidden, blocked or protected for personal reasons. This is work with the actor and myself alone. The actor can also work with an experienced company member, like Tomasz Rodowicz, who uses an instrument such as a flute to provoke and stimulate his or her inner contents of sound.

Musical 'lines of life'

How to create a composition, which comes from sound images taken from your inner musicality.

Calling

Learn calls, which are still alive in traditional cultures. These exercise the strength of the voice and teach you to go much further with the voice than the popular singer would go. To go beyond reaching the public and to contact the sound within the space.

Antiphony

How to work with a partner in antiphony by asking a question through your musical callings and sounds, to which the partner must respond. At first, this seems like a conversation without harmonization but, step by step, you discover how those exercises, in a natural way, lead you to harmonize with a partner.

Harmonization and mutuality

How to harmonize and create mutuality between two voices. The surprising effect of these exercises is that you discover that if you are in discordance you are not necessarily making a mistake. You may suddenly discover a very strong correspondence between two voices.

Indigenous musical forms

To discover other forms of music. Those which use the mutuality of voices but which do not fit our European canons, such as the *yoik* of the Sami people in Lapland.

Three voices

A system of harmonizing which introduces more partners. First, two partners keep the harmony in an interval based on fourths or fifths and the pupil has to add his or her voice in a different way. Initially finding a complementary sound, which would fit the canon, then one which would travel up and down in pitch looking for another sound altogether. This has a surprising effect – it sounds like dissonance but it actively reveals another musical system.

Interweaving the musical score with musicality

How to read an existing musical score and interweave this with the musicality discovered in the first musical step with the flute: learning how to travel from one to the other. For instance, the pupil sings a fragment of *Katolophyromai* and then immediately whispers to a partner, as if in the graveyard situation, and back again. Not in order to simply experiment, but to find the proper complexity which would reflect the subject you are dealing with.

Individuation

The pupil harmonizes with the choir then, for a brief moment, is exposed using a different means of expression (it may include movement, words, musicality, a deed, a dance, gestures); and then returns to continue the mutuality of the choir. Your task may be a practical one, as in *Avvakum*, where you may be holding the ladder leading to the tower. You may execute this action with some kind of physical sound which expresses the emotional level of the effort, then you return to the choir to sing a very precise and disciplined harmony. Bigger solos come when the actor has learnt all these steps.

Inner sounding

Inner sounding is very difficult and comes with practice with partners. For instance, when you leave the choir in order to express a situation dramatically, then the song (which you have just been singing with the others) must still be sung inside of you. It has to be continued. This is for structural reasons, of course, because the choir's song will decide how much time you have and when to return. But also because the actor is somehow on a lead and must not break it. The song inside of you can be like a demon, or it is alive inside of you like a guardian angel. It is a partner for all the other deeds and tasks which you are doing. It is the same when you are in antiphony. The song line, which was sung by the partner as a question to you, does not disappear when your partner stops singing. Your partner has interfered with your inner life with this song line and this is why you are answering. You respond to something, which still sounds inside of you. It is not as in ping pong. It is a system of penetration as in intercourse. That's why there are song lines inside you.

Reference points

I do not improvise. I have a very precise vocabulary in my work, and there always has to be a reference point within existing techniques, or in past techniques, or in life. But artists can have the ability to project, in order to connect with something, which is not visible. So you may find a reference point through your own exploration. There can be situations when you penetrate yourself with a sense that this is an experiment which leads you too far, but you still find there is something of value in it. You don't have immediate reference points, but you have to present it and continue to look for them. They will come. For instance, the musicality of breathing – I've been penetrating this technique for years, not knowing that it existed in tribal culture where it is used in a different way from the voice to express, for example, an existential reaction. The Inuit use rhythmical breathing to playfully express love or excitement.

First harmony

If you know how to deal with musicality, then you know how to create *harmonia prima*, the 'first harmony'. This means that you know not just how to produce sounds, but how to connect them, how to associate them with everything that is going on around you. You can come by this through practice.

To believe in the first harmony is very idealistic. It is to believe that certain sounds purify, bring catharsis and have a powerful 'causing' effect. Once you reach this sound, you don't have to do anything more! It is rather like the idea of the permanent idealistic unity. Is it only an abstract intellectual idea for me? No, I am searching for it in all of my performances.

I look for happiness in the theatre and I have believed all my life that it doesn't emerge through a process, but it happens suddenly as if you are struck, miraculously, by a harmony, a mutuality of voices, by sounds, which have a revelatory impact.

actors and acting

I am concerned with the actor who causes facts. I very much like the word 'causer' instead of 'actor'.

In Polish, a *sprawca* is a minor hooligan, someone who has caused something to happen. When the police pick you up because you have done something, they enter you on the report as being a *sprawca*, a causer: someone who did something, who has made something happen that is out of the ordinary and which has consequences. A *sprawca* causes facts, which are then followed by other facts. If you fight someone, it is not without consequences. You are punished – and something also happens to the one you fought. There is a cause and many consequences. The actor should be someone like that: obviously not someone who is a criminal, but someone who is seeking to cause a fact which has consequences, and not someone who is just speaking the lines of a text.[26]

The good causer also poses very difficult questions. Not questions in words, but questions through acting. The more difficult the questions – to the partner, to the constellation, to the music, to the acting – the more they electrify and energize. The questions cause the partner and the constellation to bristle, like the hairs on the back of a cat. Of course, the questions are put within an existing framework, which has already been prepared. Once this has happened you have the space and the time to be a *sprawca*, a causer. You have the right to make creative changes to the existing framework.

What is important for the 'causing' act is that it doesn't only serve the actor – it serves the others who are with him, next to him, after him. The causing act is for the constellation. There are very strict rules amongst hooligans. If you betray the constellation you are dead, you are a bastard, a nobody. You must forget about yourself when you do this

transformative causing act and think about how you enlighten your
partner. The actor's way of achieving the ardent act is similar to the
hooligan who wants to do something hot-blooded, surprising and
shocking. If they do not radiate in response, you just leave, because the
actor's function is to enlighten the partner.

Mutuality

I developed the 'mutuality'[27] exercises from an observation taken from
life. The crucial and most difficult things are the most simple. We see the
truth as something very simple but so difficult to achieve. I call mutuality
'the paradigm of simplicity'.

I found that the most vibrating energy and magnetic power occurs
when two people come to each other. This observation comes from a
shocking moment in a valley in Italy while I was walking to St Francis'
cave. It was early morning. Through the mist, in the far distance, on the
other side of the valley, was another figure. We could either choose to
cross each other's paths or pass each other far apart. I am a shy person –
particularly at that time, when I was about twenty years old – but I
decided that I had to meet this man. It was not a rational decision. A
rational mind would tell you not to meet this man because hell knows
who he is! He was probably a local man and I was a lost foreigner in this
emptiness, but I decided to meet him. He felt the same, and as we
approached each other something happened in each couple of steps: the
magnetism of two people coming closer and closer, reverberating. Then
we met. It was a significant meeting. The paradox was that I could hardly
speak Italian and he didn't speak another language but we understood
each other perfectly.

He did some karate training with me. Here were two beings who
removed their shirts, and with our half-naked bodies we followed each
other's gestures. It was a beautiful dance of effort, sweat, breathing.
Breathing was the language between us.

When I came to Gardzienice, I started to develop a training based on
a successive form of interaction in which two people can be close to each
other and then leave. This is the beginning of theatre. A dialogue between
two beings. It doesn't have to be another person – you can meet a ghost.

You are coming to each other and leaving, coming and going. Everything happens within this paradigm. You create aesthetics. The way you perceive when you are close to each other is different to when you are further away. Love happens, of course, because your emotions confront the emotions of the other. Love doesn't only mean intercourse. When we talk about the marriage of heaven and earth, then we think about an exchange of energy.

When the first action happens, the most significant thing occurs: you read the other being. When I came close to this man, I was reading him, and vice versa. We followed words from the same book, we were two parts of the same poem.

This training has enormous potential. In our theatre work this training is always between two people *as they are*. They read each other and create through each other forms, moves, turns and bows. You can achieve very refined, even acrobatic results with mutuality but this training is based on how the person is. For example, take Mariusz Gołaj. *His* body, *his* tempo, *his* ability, *his* potential. I deposited this exploration of mutuality with Mariusz and his partners. Over the years they were just themselves, but they developed something that was particular to the characteristics of their own bodies.

When we entered the recent work on *Metamorphoses*, I decided to go further with mutuality – to refer our mutuality to those figures which were captured and created by the artists in ancient times. I started to study paintings and sculptures of two beings in mutual relation to each other. In *Metamorphoses* I tried to work through analogies and comparison to see how much of this work belongs to antiquity, how much the mutuality which can be found in antiquity's aesthetics can initiate, inspire and retrieve from you. Both ways. Some poses which belonged to the original mutuality training could be found in antiquity.

The philosophy of the ancients was also based on mutuality – on Socratic dialogue. Then I found something else: shame. Shame can be understood as modesty, uncertainty, something which is natural to children. You can see it on their faces when something has touched the secrecy of their inner life. It is like a feather inside you which is fragile. Following Plato, I believe that this is about your soul.

You cannot create mutuality if you are shameless. Plato tells us that ethics are based on shame. You have to respect it because if you become shameless you cannot be an actor.

❖ Sami people

(From an interview with Peter Hulton for Arts Archives in 1993)

In Lapland, amongst the Sami people, I found that which I had considered to be my own obsession existed as a fully developed technique, the yoik, which included and connected all the sounds of the emotions and the psyche. The sounds of those parts of our lives, which we never reveal as a society. The Sami's technique is serious, creative and musical.

I believe that every culture had its own yoik. It is just that the Sami people have kept it; they have not destroyed or crushed it. It has been kept in a very developed form. Every culture had its own yoik, and still has it, but in many instances it is scattered throughout the culture and exists only as a residue, a reminder of something that no longer fits.

Yoikers have a very particular way of expressing what they do with the voice. They never say they are singing. They say they are 'yoiking'. What does this mean? Usually when we sing, we sing about something. They say, rather, that they are 'yoiking some-thing'. So I am yoiking tree in the forest. I am not yoiking about the tree. I am yoiking tree. I am yoiking heaven. I am yoiking grass. I am yoiking wind. I am yoiking wolf. I am yoiking you. You are sitting in front of me and I can try to yoik you, to evoke you. This does not mean that I improvise a song about you or that I try to describe you. It means, in my terms, that I am reading you. But it is a particular way of reading, in which I am not thinking about you so much as somehow sculpting you, trying to touch the spaces, the shapes of you, your measurement, your softness or hardness, your height, your nerves . . . I am yoiking you and, for the Sami people, this is a way of reading people, reading wolf, reading wind. For me, this technique of yoiking was an incredible discovery.

Moreover, they say that yoik has no beginning and no end. Songs usually have a beginning and an end. Yoik never has a beginning and an end . . . it follows the path of wholeness. As when we read a human being, we do not start from the beginning of each of us. We simply do not know where our beginning is, or our end.

There are key words within our working processes. Two such words are 'reading' and 'mutuality'. Our work is partner to partner and what I have said about yoik is mutuality. I have to read my partner. I read a book. The book may take me on a journey. The journey can be very concrete if there is song and music behind it. There can be mutuality of the voice, the coming of one to the other. If I am trying to come into my partner's singing through my own voice, intertwined with his voice, resonance, dynamic and rhythm, then it is as if my partner is creating life in my body. At that moment, mutuality is of the highest order. ❖

A sensitive actor can be in mutuality with partners when they reach a certain level of mutuality and touching. But on the administrative stage, the sense is often only communicated through words. In our performances, the sense is transferred to the acting partner through other means of expression. The penetration of the partner is more complex and the demands made on the partner are more challenging.

Training is most important with mutuality. It allows you to find the best possible alchemy between partners. When you fix the relationship between acting partners solely on the level of words, it is like Western trading. Trading can be on a very aseptic level, as in the supermarkets in the West. But trading can go much further if we consider, for example, the Middle Eastern countries, where trading is an art. It is part of the culture to penetrate another person, to know as much as possible about him or her and, through this knowledge, to discover more about yourself. In this archetypical system of trading there are all the complexities, which belong to human expression. There are gestures, subtext, moves towards and away. Offers which are multiplied in different ways to test whether the offer two minutes earlier was more correct than this latest one. You have to play with the space around the partner. It is an incredible theatre, which is like an opera sung by two people, touching the complex means of human expression.

In the Western supermarket, everything is eliminated. You take the goods from the shelves, you put them in the basket, pay the bill and go away. This is like simply exchanging lines in administrative theatre. This is the difference and it is the same with the mutual act: it is more like the archetypical ritualistic process, which is still alive in Asia and in the Middle East.

Partnership

Partnership defines all the other exercises. In every situation where one body enters a space, another one joins it and they come close to each other, all the processes are ignited. Those of recognition, of comparison. The first revelatory exercise in my work is when two actors enter the space from opposite sides and they meet and they leave the space and then come again and meet. This is such a powerful process, you don't have to give them any other task.

It continues when you give the actors the task of comparing themselves to each other, of recognizing yourself through the other. I call this 'reading the partner'. This exchange involves touching. The word 'touch' comes from the Latin *tactus*, which means 'rhythm'. Touching immediately opens a large sphere between two people – opening and describing their mysterious inner world of the self.

This exercise based on meeting is a paradigm of curiosity. The results of these meetings occur on a number of levels: the meeting can be like a story, which says something about everyone but also about the two of them. It can also lead to a narrative or thematic situation, which uncovers the hidden potential of the actors. This would normally take a long time to reveal through an acting process, which intends to 'unblock' the actor.

'Unblocking' is bullshit. It is just a presumption of a director or trainer that they have the key to open different doors. I have seen so many dramas and misunderstandings with people who have no talent, no eye, no feeling to open anything whatsoever in another person. That's why I don't believe in this theory of unblocking or opening. I just want two human beings with a predisposition for acting to meet together and leave. This process of walking in and out says more than any interference of a director, trainer or guru into the training of an actor.

The biggest philosophical and theatrical problem is the first encounter between two human beings because humanity has constructed the first encounter as a conflict. In our literature, when the aliens arrive, we predict conflict. This is a huge philosophical, mental, emotional problem for me. I want to turn it into its opposite because, in an encounter of this kind, my nature wishes to express gratitude, to adore and accept, to find the other more interesting than myself. I try to transform into the other being in order to know more about myself and to evaluate this knowledge.

The mutuality exercise

This process of mutuality[28] has several stages:

The first encounter

This is repeated several times in a common rhythm to enable both actors to be involved in a common process without any anticipation. Face to face, body to body, arms to arms, cheek to cheek. The actors enter the room and leave, but impressions are already forming, as when you read the first sentences of a book.

The actor is a living book

Of course the actors have to be in a state of concentration and without any preconcept, without anticipation or intention. This is a reading process: when you read a book you have some expectations, but if you are imposing your own expectations you will close the book immediately, because it will never fulfil them.

Compact energy

In the next stage of the process they stay in front of each other in a position of compact energy, ready to go further with slightly bent knees, relaxed hands and arms and with a relaxed, wandering head. The senses are open. The partners do not steer each other. They are in a paradoxical situation of being passive but at the same time ready to act. They are attentive. The bent-knee position has been known since man became a hunter, but the arms in permanent relaxation is unusual. I do not allow the head and arms to engage until the appropriate moment because the head and arms in our culture are the parts of the body which immediately behave in clichés and want to say something, which does not necessarily reflect what is inside you. The periphery of the body prevents you from working from the inside.

The paradigm of shame

At the moment when the partners know what they want to say, the first move of the hands is very significant and so fully harmonized with their inner statement that it is often revelatory in the most surprising way. The actor stands in front of the partner breast to breast, pelvis to pelvis. Sometimes the head can be turned a little to keep your partner in focus, but not to the extent that you are leading them. The head can also be slightly down, as an expression of uncertainty or expression of shame. This paradigm of shame is very important. It is like a child who is brought into a new situation where the first reaction might be uncertainty, shame, modesty, and the first question is asked: Am I invited or not?

(Sometimes it happens that there is no impulse to return again to a second encounter. It is immediately clear that between these two actors there is no alchemy, that there will be a negative friction between them.)

Back to back

The partners re-enter the space and turn their backs to each other, then turn back to face each other and they leave. This is repeated, but when they are back to back they delicately touch and this is the first moment of recognition, which is based on the purity of their in-tentions. It occurs back to back because in the intimacy of front to front, premeditated concepts and inappropriate sexual tendencies can impose. The amount of information, which comes with this first touch, is unbelievable.

Eroticism is necessary to theatre, it comes from Eros and Dionysus and if you expel eroticism from the theatre it is only propaganda. Eros signified eroticism. I am not referring to intercourse. The encounter has to be on the pre-mature level, before the human being came to understand what Eros means.

Lifting

Then they leave the space again, come again, and turn back to back and lean on each other. Then again, and this time they lift each other, back to back. They are saying, 'I am holding you, you are mine, I promise you safety, I promise you everything I can in the most simple way.' That is the first moment of encounter, with sympathy.

The first touch

They make physical contact, there is a little lift and the one being elevated feels very comfortable. This is repeated so that this comfort is perfectly provided. Then they make the first move of the arm and the head, which is the first recognition of another element: the touching of a given point of the body of your partner. This is the first gesture, as in the darkness when you hold out your hand and you try to find out what is there. The moment that you touch in this way your impressions are without any preconceptions, causing strong intellectual and emotional processes to occur. This first touch might be done with closed eyes, particularly with those actors who have difficulty in quietening their minds.

Touch of recognition

The next touch has to be done with proper timing so that it reflects the rhythm of the breathing. Through these touches you are sculpting what you recognize from this experience. Metaphorically this is the shape, the vibrations, the temperature and the chemistry, which tell you what you are dealing with. At the same time it enables each person to read his or her own state of being. The partners leave and return and the other repeats this exchange. The receiving partner reacts because the touches are very sensitive and cause a response.

Forming the partner

Through this very subtle, pre-mature system of recognition you create the potential of the partner's body because the body reacts and it means that the actors are already building figures. One actor sculpts their partner's body while they respond in one sense as if they are asleep, in that they move only in relation to the strength of your touch. They are ready to respond naturally to the point of contact. They have to make their body weightless, transparent without any resistance, opening its senses and its ability to react in the most subtle, delicate action. The actor forms the partner but it doesn't mean that the partner is helpless or without any will. They are dancing the same dance. If you touch a leaf on a tree, you touch delicately but it doesn't mean that it doesn't move because you didn't see it. Every touch causes movement. Every action causes a reaction. It is not simply a physiological reaction; it is a psycho-somatic reaction.

Touching centres

Each actor touches centres, which are the sources of movement. There are points within the body which are more sensitive – where the meridians cross on the hips, for example, or the joints. There is a map of common points and a map of more unusual points. Once the actor finds some of the unusual points within their partner's body, they are beginning to read their psychosomatics very deeply (that is, if theirs is a life-penetrating intelligence and not a vulgar intelligence). The intelligence has to be sympathetic because the actor is not doing this to instrumentalize their partner but to make his or her 'flower' flourish. Suddenly you can see that someone's inner aura radiates. Zeami was calling this the 'flower', but he developed this within whole processes, whereas I see the 'flower' within this elementary exercise.

Rhythmicized breathing

The partners have to rhythmicize the breathing in a natural way. The first representation of the voice is through the breath. This process involves the emotions although it is disciplined. Then the first notes of sounding occur. Every touch is like a sound, and then (following this process) they compose a musical core, which has to be perfectly synchronized with the line of life of the body. This process enables the actors to develop more complex imagery.

Iconograms

Iconograms are the living, moving and singing tableaux which evolve in relation to mutuality training and historical research.

Rules of iconograms:

1   The iconograms refer to existing patterns within the given arts of an historical period.

A sequence from mutuality training, 2003. Mariusz Gołaj and Dorota Porowska. *Photo*: Gardzienice Archive.

Above and left: A sequence from mutuality training, 2003. Mariusz Gołaj and Elżbieta Rojek. *Photo*: Gardzienice Archive.

2   There are two partners in an exercise in which one initiates the other. The roles are then reversed.

3   Music and rhythm influence the structure. For example, the actors may be given the task of sculpting each other within four beats.

In the stage of pre-maturity within these first encounters, the actors have not yet been referred to the given background, and yet they may create surprisingly similar poses and gestures which can be found in the history of art. I work for a long time on this stage until some significant representations of those figures and postures emerge. Then I ask the actors to refer to books and discover the surprising similarity between their own work and those from the history of art. Then we work on the iconograms that create a chain of pictures, which are the line of life of the body. They are then ready to be used within the performance.

Historical references

The mutuality exercises were developed in relation to four main historiocultural spheres, the first being indigenous European culture which, for me, is within a trajectory from Chagall to Brueghel: the rural culture of Brueghel and the fantasy and folk influences of Chagall. The second was Orthodox iconography – the East European, Russian and Greek. I drew upon popular icons from a huge range of anonymous artists all the way to Rublow. The third sphere was that of the Middle Ages and the way in which the human body was presented in the woodcuts and manuscripts of the period. For example, *Fortuna* from the Beuron manuscript.[29] The fourth was the ancient Greek culture, with particular reference to the vase paintings mainly from the sixth to fourth centuries BC.

Subtlety of the body

The mutuality training makes your body responsive. The way the body is taught to react and to form different pictograms gives the actor a certain subtlety. It also teaches the actor to create the pictograms when the body is involved in continuous rhythmical action. This action is ignited, initiated and formed by the partner, directly through his or her hands and body. You are placed in the hands and imagination of your partner. Through the sensibility of the other actor, your moves are directed through his or her actions towards your body. This creates a completely different chemistry, lightness, transparency and subtlety. The quality and texture of the body movement is created through this work.

Touching and sculpting

Imagine someone who falls in a faint and someone next to him tries to revive him and holds him up, supporting and returning him to a dignified position. She brings him to standing and firms his hands, and the one who is revived is immediately brought back and refreshed as if nothing has happened. Then again he has weak legs but this time his helper brings him back, firming his head, which brings him back to steadiness. The helper is forming, firming and sketching the body of the other. 'Weak legs' is characteristic of the partner who is being formed; the one who is initiating is dancing out the images through the body of the partner.

The body constantly in motion

This operation has to be very disciplined – within the correct timing and rhythm. The musicality is 'done' by those who are acting on a primal level using the breath. You sing a song of the body. All the time the body is in motion, neither slow or fast but reflecting the rhythm of the breath. If, instead of the breathing, you are using song, you can change the body tempo depending on the rhythm of the song. This is important because the most effective thinking is when the body is in motion. The temperature of the body increases, the brain functions more efficiently. Being in a constant state of movement trains you to be present in each moment with a full sense of awareness. The partner's energy is very important, because it alarms and sharpens your energy and your process of thinking. You are never lost, because there is someone like a good spirit at your side, who surprises and challenges you. You exchange roles quite quickly, and this shifting operation creates a high level of understanding of your shared direction.

The procedure of mutuality, made rhythmical by the punctuation of the breathing, or by the sounds based on the score of the breathing, is further enriched by the musical lines. Mutuality has one indispensable value, which is that it is a dynamic manoeuvre in motion. Stillness in the

Above and left: Iconograms inspired by images from ancient Greek vases (satyr dances), 2003. Elżbieta Rojek. *Photo*: Gardzienice Archive.

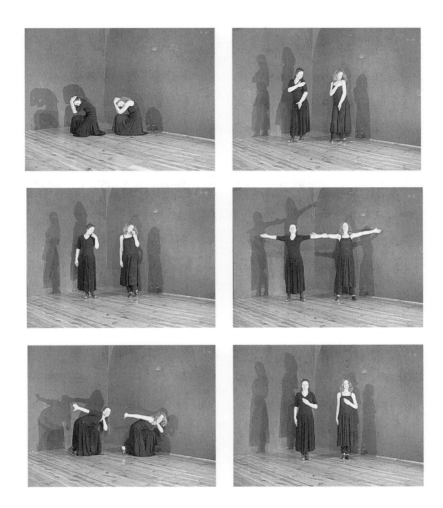

Above and left: Gestures (*chieronimia*) in preparation for a new performance based on the work of Euripides, 2003. *Left to right*: Joanna Holcgreber and Anna Helena McLean. *Photo*: Gardzienice Archive.

history of art is just the captured image of life's dynamics. That's why, in the project that led to *Metamorphoses*, I was able to animate the iconography of ancient Greek paintings – to let them move, escape from the vase, continue the dance within their own momentum.

There has to be movement. Painters can only reconstruct the dynamic process of life, they are suffering and dancing around their empty canvas before they make each line because they are trying to capture dynamic moment. And life is never frozen. That's my attitude: to catch the critical moment of life, that moment when the Mona Lisa smiled.

Concluding

The conclusion of this work is not made by an outside, cold observer who records the work like a mirror or a director. It is done through the synchronized action of two partners who have found and proved that a sequence works for both of them working within the same process. When two can prove that something is truthful it can be accepted. When only one is proving that something is truthful, it is in danger of being a pretension, or an imposition, or simply an opinion.

Training

For each new theatre project it is necessary to prepare new lines of life, new aesthetics for the voice and body. The majority of the training methods are carefully developed and verified by time. They form the letters of an exercise alphabet which I apply in practical work. Obviously, body and voice exercises keep the actor fit and maintain a level of performance skill. But I want to stress that they can have considerable contribution to one's health, both mental and physical. Through this kind of training, the actor can get acquainted with herself.

The partnership work can also help this process where the actor can not only develop a deep understanding of the partner but also gain greater knowledge, through the partner, of herself. This is mutuality. In such practice it is impossible to avoid the boundary between work which serves theatre and work which serves the human being. On the one hand we are dealing with the joy of movement – aspiring towards lightness, dreaming about flying – and on the other, when we work in pairs, we cannot stop wondering about each other. In the joyful dynamics of approaching and departing, in antiphony, in the quasi-gymnastics in which we are constantly surprised by the stream of new images of our partner, new figures, gestures, aspects of the other person, in the running towards and away, in whirling, lifting, jumping, we reach a certain level of synchronicity. In all these moments we stop perceiving the activity as acrobatics. We only think in terms of metaphors. It is as if we were dancing poetry.

And then we want to be better – for the other person, for our partner, for the one with whom our body is synchronized. We want to be better than we are because we have to be more considerate, humble and precise. We cannot make mistakes because it can be physically harmful.

The very nature of 'causing an effect' in each other is a purifying process, offering a sense of a happy encounter with another person together with a harmonious conclusion. Within the stream of encounters, increasingly sophisticated manoeuvres evolve; even violent and aggressive gestures occur which are acceptable within the form. It is like fencing, when those who cross their swords know that their thrusts cannot hurt. There has to be playfulness. This kind of dynamic flexibility of the body cannot be approached ostentatiously or with pompous seriousness. There has to be space for fun, for chance, as well as incident. Nothing can be forced from a partner. It can only be drawn out, evoked, as if calling the partner. This calling has to elicit an adequate answer. This is antiphony – a dialogue of call and response.

Morning exercises

As I have said, working with the body in our training is a form of health practice. From the very beginning at the Centre for Theatre Practices we have cultivated a belief that one should start the day with physical exercises. These exercises should take place outdoors, in an open space, in relation to nature. It is not only a matter of breathing fresh air, awakening your body to life, unblocking bio-energy, or ultimately experiencing the joy of exercising together, although all these aspects are significant. It is a matter of energy, which is of a completely different nature to that experienced indoors.

Energy broadens our inner space, our 'uncultivated garden' in which our body lives, and allows more beautiful flowers to bloom. Perhaps it is partly because our inner life is influenced by our perception of the landscape, astonishing skies, wind on our skin, sound of birdsong, smell of the earth, and all our senses are exercised in this process.

The morning exercises are intended to be difficult and demanding. They encourage us to be brave. They provoke us. First of all they have to guarantee safety. So we focus on assisting the partner, offering safe arms, secure contact. Everyone within the group has to fully concentrate even if they are not actively involved in the immediate physical exchange. It is a situation in which there is both movement, concentration and concentration in movement.

The rest of the group has to be ready to make an assisting movement or gesture. This form of attention evokes a sense in those assisting that the same exercise lives in them, provoking inner animation. It enables you to assimilate the movement, to make one, two, three steps and to stretch out your hands at precisely the right moment, to support the acrobatic move. But it also allows your body to foresee, instinctively, a moment of danger, threat or fall.

The purpose of these exercises is also to focus on the way in which the body finds itself in the most unexpected positions. So the acrobatic training is very dynamic and teaches the actor how to both find and freeze the momentum in the most unexpected and surprising, vital kinetic movement.

Night running

My father was a very speedy man. I will always hear, to the end of my life, the way in which he ran up the stairs in our house. I always remember running as a moment of being very happy. Either that, or I was running in order to become happy. Night running is probably about happiness.

After introducing this as part of the daily life of the group, I began to do some research, and discovered that running is a ritual in many cultures, or that it functions like a ritual. I made a great effort for many years to experience such a ritual and I went to Mexico to Sierra

Madre Occidental, to Tarahumara country, to visit the Indian tribe there. I participated in the Raramuri running practice with the Indians.

Running is a *petite mort* – a small death – like making love. It brings you to a climax and at the same time to the border of life. When you run for happiness and happiness is never accessible, you run faster, you chase, but happiness runs away from you. Instead of capturing happiness you are touching death because you touch the extremes: the extremity of your breath, of your physical opportunities and possibilities. Achilles' pursuit of Hector around the walls of Troy belongs to the same symbolic sphere.

It is very practical. Your breathing is altered and your muscles are stretched. Your mind is also affected: you experience the way the landscape is passing, and you are no longer *observing* but *perceiving* the things that you pass. The amount of detail which you perceive and the impact you are getting from experience is completely different.

I am not talking about running around the streets of New York. I am talking about Gardzienice's meadows, forest, or (with the Tarahumara) through canyons, along the rocky paths where they run day and night. The practice in which I took part was sixteen hours of non-stop running.

Two teams run. I was only able to run for some dozen minutes and then I collapsed but they came back after about 12 kilometres (7 miles) and I tried to join them again. A lot of things happen during the running that belong to ritualistic practice. To some it looks like a sport, but for me it is a transcendent ritual, a sort of mystery.

Running is an extremely realistic, existential practice and it can also be a sort of rehearsal. If you introduce different moves, different gestures and exercises during the running, they are more realistic, but at the same time they incorporate 'figures'. So the practice becomes artistic and aesthetic.

The group is anything between eight and twenty people. Not a crowd because then the chemistry is bad and it cannot be stimulated properly. The leader, as in the ancient Greek choir, proposes the theme, the subject, the exercises of the voice, the theatrical momentum. An existential physiological act, which is very realistic, becomes artistic, aesthetic. It can become almost mystical. Suddenly the ground is not the ground, but something like a mystical ladder which you are climbing. There are emotions within the group which can affect you deeply.

Running can create an incredible pulsation of the given song that we are working on in the training. This pulsation is rhythmicized and evokes voices which would never be evoked in a static situation within a theatre space. Because you pump your diaphragm, you open your throat and it happens naturally. You don't have to use artificial methods. You are naturally opening yourself and you hear the song in a way that would be unreachable on the stage. That's why I have introduced the audible pulse of breathing in the performance, which is a reflection of the running.

Transcending your culture

Ideally, the expeditions are where the actor is learning to perceive. It is an art, and is much deeper than just looking.

In the early expeditions the cultural references were often Gypsies. We were not so much taking themes from their dances, but certain electrifying gestures – a hand movement – that seemed a particularly significant expression of a person through their body. The gesture was already found. The actor is seeing the crux of this gesture as a separate phenomenon, not as a part of the whole body. Through the training process, I would encourage an actor to 'exercise' this gesture and to reorganize all the dynamics of the rest of the body around it so that the gesture is a source for the rest of the movement. It means somehow to re-compose the body, to teach the body new dynamics which are influenced by this gesture, then to sculpt the actor.

The actor is always starting with the particularity of their own culture. But then you are working in the way that is in reference to that which is old, ancient, forgotten or hidden, which can mean it is somehow universal. The actor has to have the ability to transcend his or her own culture. If somebody is saying, 'But I am Swedish and that's me!', I am saying it means that you are limiting yourself. All that you can do is probably only possible within the constraints of today. It means that you are nothing else but a replica of a contemporary cliché. Ideally, I am going further, not only demanding that the actor transcends their own culture, but transcends their own sex.

Real 'acting out' occurs when the man is able to break through the limitation of his male conditions and assumptions to reach the secret and the enigma of the female body. Of course you cannot get it without identifying with the female soul, and vice versa. This is the old knowledge of Eastern theatre and of ancient Greek theatre, but now it is extremely difficult to reach it. Through transcending your own state and culture, you have much more knowledge about what you have just broken through.

The constellation

Another word which is important for me is 'constellation'. Not everyone can be in mutual relation with everyone else. That is why the way of putting people together in an ensemble, finding and creating a proper constellation is fundamental to our work. This is why I prefer to use the word 'gatherer' for a function such as mine.

The opposite of the actor's personal work is the work within the constellation. I collect people not only to have certain figures and characters but also to have a kind of garden which blossoms in a special way, and which is able to produce a special sort of chemistry. I look for constellations of people. Gardzienice's performances are created so infrequently because I am waiting for the moment when the constellation will be complete.

My theatrical model of the constellation of actors on stage relates to the dithyramb. The 'art of dithyramb' exists when this and no another constellation of people is able to express this and no other issue, subject or theme, with the proper energy, with the proper chemistry, and with the proper dynamics. I am referring not only to that which is spoken, but the way of creating the whole world with the body, music and space. And you could say, for example, 'Yes, but without one of your actors – for example, Mariana – it would still be the same performance.' No. It would be the same performance, but not the same issue.

Our group could be recognized as a collective but this is not the case. In performance, there is always the chorus or choir from which the individual actor emerges. But within the group, everyone is an unrepeatable individual who gets an opportunity to develop, while retaining a responsibility to the message which the constellation has to reveal. It is the same in life as it is in the performance.

In the first scenes of *Avvakum*, when the common body comes with the message of exile, I asked the actors to make their voices and the way they shaped their bodies individual to such an extent that each was immediately recognizable as a separate line of life, identifiable through the rest of the performance.

Finding this distinction is the hardest work. It is a straightforward task to create a collective scene. You introduce proper training, everybody is doing the same, as in dance or chorus, but that's not the point. Within this collective, there is variety which you sometimes see amongst flying seagulls. Seagulls are together, but they never fly together. You see this individualization all the time: they practise in different ways their common nature of flying, using all their means of expression.

Antiphony

Antiphony is a way of singing which is based on a question-and-answer situation. I observed this on Mount Athos in Greece, where the monks sing in this way.

If there is no antiphony, it means that the actor didn't question his partner in such a way that it would oblige him or her to answer. In my work, the actors practise antiphony through the voice and body. You don't have to question using words, but through gesture, sound or touch. It is about questioning your partner as deeply as possible to get his or her revelatory reaction. And, of course, when your partner is asking such intense questions, this may strip you down. Suddenly you are naked and you have to react as a naive, naked person. This operation is learnt within the training. It is between the actor and me. I am the one who is in antiphony. Metaphorically, I am the woman for the man and the man for the woman, let's say. The first partner.

My task is to find out, to read what is organically tuned inside the actor – where are the notes, the musical code, the sounds of music, its accentuation and its rhythm, and how can these be called upon.

Sometimes there are surprises. Some partners fall into a communion whose origins are not immediately identifiable, but which create a fascinating affair. They are not falling in love with each other, but they are creating a chemistry between themselves. This inspires their own invention. In such a situation, I can only watch and adjust and show in which fields we are moving. They are already in full antiphony.

The third actor

Everything that I have said so far could lead you to the conclusion that we are working with a Stanislavskian 'fourth wall'. It is not the case. I always incorporate a third person who assists two partners involved in an intimate scene. This third actor represents the public, but also takes the public into consideration because this figure is not only a watcher but also an intruder into the action of the event and its momentum. It is almost impossible for actors to do it truthfully, because when they deal with the public they immediately play to the public. This tendency concerns their psychology, which they have to overcome in order for the scene to be very intimate and at the same time have to accept the intruder.

Who is this third actor? The third actor is a servant, an intruder, a third voice. A creator of 'destructive dissonance'. The staring eye of the public. An almost invisible guardian angel, an assistance-giver and one who leaves the process between two partners, wishing them to fail. He is Caliban, an unleashed devil. A Good Samaritan who can offer the shirt off his back while he is shamelessly naked and ready to share his last crumb. He is a man for a woman and a woman for a man, identifying in one moment with the partners, and judging and condemning in the next. The third actor is the one who both rings the bell and is the bell itself. He or she *plays*.

I don't believe that it is truthful if you pretend that there is no public. This is the case with some false theatres, which pretend that they are performing a mystery, which is like a religious mass for them. It is as if the audience is behind a glass wall. Why? The real rituals between the indigenous tribal people always accept the public, even play with public.

The multiplied actor

In the so-called bourgeois city theatre, the cast list in the programme describes who is who. For example, Armand the lover, the first stupid servant woman, the princess, the drunkard. Actors in nineteenth-century theatre played types. They were unified in this way. They played roles adequate to the types they represented as human beings; it very much relied on their physical appearance. Somehow it still functions today.

In every actor there is an immeasurable amount of potential and possibility. You can overcome your image – it's just a question of finding the way to metamorphose your personality. There is also a difference between an actor who is just speaking his lines and one who is dealing with realities. I have to make a comparison with the situation of the warrior on the battlefield. When the actor is on the stage he is immediately facing his enemies: the public and all that surrounds him. His task is to fight against them. He is armed and uses his tools of expression as a sword. He has to be angry. Imagine a world in which you fight with many enemies. Every turn is to another enemy, representing another reality, another text, another way of expression. The actor deals with different potential, fights first with a big man, then turns to one who is very fast, a third who is tricky. Each demands a different way of being, a different text. You are using the same words, you have the same body, but the way in which you are metamorphosing your means of expression is totally transforming you.

This reflects the idea of 'becoming'. You use one text and you suggest many subtexts. One body suggesting and expressing many bodies. It is the art of transformation, of course.

The stage should be a battlefield and the actor should be a sword-fighter who fights many enemies at the same time, so her energy, her presence has to be multiplied and changeable. When I refer to the battlefield I don't mean anything militaristic at all. It's about the highest possible equilibrium, means of expression that are trained in such an extreme way that they can express polyphony instead of monody. Actors are basically monodic – one word, one picture, one image. Today we say, 'Whatever he plays, we see him.' I would say, 'No. The actor is great when his ability of metamorphosis is so strong that he himself is not visible, and disappears.'

Repetition

If something has been discovered, trained and fixed as a meaningful element of the given scene in a performance, it has to be trained continuously to keep it on the proper level. In this I am closer to music than to theatre and acting. Concert musicians know how dangerous it is not to train, and how easily – even if you are a great artist – you can get out of tune. So they train all the time, concentrating especially on difficult passages. The actor has to do the same.

I believe that a certain momentum can create a *causing effect*, giving rise to mysterious results and consequences. Certain gestures, tunes, turns of the body have to be done precisely, because they are causing a special chemistry to which partners must react properly and to which the public must also respond. The audience easily recognizes when something has lost its correct momentum.

To reach the correct momentum you have to train a particular means of expression repetitively – whether it is the voice, the gesture, a certain movement or a moment of harmony.

When people talk about theatre there is often much glibness because theatre seems to give people the idea that it is all about freedom of expression. The actor declares, 'I am expressing myself!' What does it mean, 'I am expressing myself'? It means, 'Today I feel like this, another day I feel that.' In music this is not the case, nor is it in dance. Because the feeling is something else; it is like an angel above you. So make the angel open the wings, but your body, your voice, your gesture, has to be precisely to the tune, to the point.

You can try to make a system out of the process of artistic work. But the system is only as good as the extent to which it can keep the work within the discipline you have prescribed. When actors have to solve a problem, they often have to work beyond their methodology. In some situations it is evident that their methodology no longer works. In the face of a particular challenge, it just produces clichés. My advice is, don't work methodologically. If you do follow a method you are killing the work itself, and then you can only work in order to demonstrate. You can never retrieve the actor's organic potential.

section four | **performance**

theatre composition

It is necessary to see ourselves within the patterns of history. The artist is not so concerned with the evolution of mankind, but the evolution of oneself. This is something that you must be concerned with as an artist and as a human being. The theme and literary work that I choose as a reference point for each new performance has to be explained within the context of where we were in that specific moment of time in our lives and our history. All the material which I refer to may seem very exotic and without any relation to our own problems. For example, the historical texts of Apuleius' *The Golden Ass* and *The Life of the Archpriest Avvakum*. But these books were reflecting situations which occurred in contemporary life.

I choose such 'exotic' material rather than a contemporary script because it reflects the same problem on a larger scale. If, for instance, you see that you are living in a social or political climate which was similar to a period in history, you are better able to understand yourself because this historical reference provides a broader perspective.

It is important to realize that human processes are cyclical in nature and have a tendency to repeat themselves. This understanding is more influential on your credo as an artist and as a human being than the modern emphasis on progress is willing to reveal. It allows you to better understand the mechanism of the changes which are taking place. The future is easier to predict because you know what the options were in the past under similar circumstances. It allows you to make better choices.

106 performance ■

Performance 1: *Avvakum*

The problem of Russia

How do you look for your identity? The material I select relates to this investigation, which concerns the heritage of my soul, the heritage of my mind, my people, and my context. Of course, in the context of the particular relationship between Russia and Poland, every Pole is exploring this somehow.

In 1981 and in 1983, Communism broke a little: it was the time of Solidarity and then afterwards came martial law. At the time, I thought that there were three main problems facing human nature in this geographical zone: freedom, God and Russia. Russia pretended to be the Third Rome – the empire that could rule the world and possess the mind and soul with its ideology. At the time, I said that the most important of these three problems was Russia because the long hands of Moscow reached out to us. I looked for a source book which spoke most resonantly about the Russian soul, the Russian nature.

There is nothing more representative than *The Life of the Archpriest Avvakum*.[30] Avvakum was a significant historical character living in seventeenth-century Russia who wrote a personal testimony. He recorded his life in vivid, theatrical circumstances. He was imprisoned and testified to his colleague, Fiodor – with whom he had, I believe, a platonic love/hate affair. They were in two separate cells, there was a wall between them, and they argued and quarrelled. Avvakum spoke about his life and Fiodor recorded his words.

The language of his autobiography is very vivid. His style is dynamic, energizing, colourful, dramatic, expressive, lurid, pictorial and poetic. It has a large musical range, going from the highest C down to the lowest F. This piece combines so-called high culture with so-called low culture because it is written in the manner of the biographies of the saints. Avvakum was well educated, he knew the Bible perfectly, as well as the lives of the saints and the lives of the desert fathers. He was knowledgeable about Western and Orthodox Christianity. But at the same time the vitality in his writing leads him to 'explosions'. Suddenly he uses the language of primitive people. If he hadn't been a monk, a priest, a prophet, a hermit, if he hadn't devoted himself to religion, he would have been a poet or writer. He quotes the sayings belonging to folklore. He invents, but at the same time he uses words, even curses, that have such a strong emotional dynamic that they tear and burn the pages as you read them.

The book is written 'on the road' from Moscow to Siberia in a number of dialects. Avvakum had lived in many parts of Russia and he had an ability to identify with the given language. This signifies a great artist like Dante, who revolutionized Italian by using the language of the lower classes. The same goes for Villon and Rabelais.

The Life of Archpriest Avvakum became the source book for modern Russian literature. This book has incredible potential for theatre: it is built on a situation of dialogue and polyphony which was so ingeniously analysed by Bakhtin.

Avvakum expresses the contradictions in the extremes of behaviour of the time. This frightens many rationalist Western Europeans, but it is so profitable for theatre and art. Life is close to the truth when tears are close to laughter; when pride is switched into humility. In this religious context, the emotional and spiritual life of the human being is transparent, vibrating, transforming.

The expeditions

In the early stages of work, I try to establish links between the theme, the subject, the philosophy, and the challenge with the cultural and natural environment. *The Life of Archpriest Avvakum* raises questions about freedom, the contradiction between common duty and individuality within the system, and questions concerning Euro-Asian culture. Expeditions were made to those communities where you can find relics of this Euro-Asian mentality.

The Łemko are part of a geographical zone in the Carpathian Mountains where there was a mixture of cultures: Polish, Ukrainian, Slovakian people together with Jews, Gypsies and Armenians. Tragically, during the war many of these communities were exterminated and expelled from this land, but in people's memories the echo of those times when they lived together are still alive. These people are in between two huge religious worlds: the Eastern Orthodox and the Western Latin. The Łemko had been able to incorporate both because they belonged to the Graeco-Roman church, which absorbed both elements. Both had invaded them, but they adapted. Their souls are Eastern but their minds are Western.

Training

It is in the nature of the performance to establish a new training, which specifically reflects the given subject that we are working with and generates a new aesthetic. The new training leads to a specific body language and form of vocal work.

From each expedition we bring observations, pictures, smells, images of living. This is the pre-performance work. At a later stage, in constructing the performance, I build images and tableaux in which actors were composed appropriately to the content. They were like living pictures: static in one moment, and in the next very alive, metamorphosing, changing the composition, filling the space with life.

Studying iconography

When preparing *Avvakum* we referred to the indigenous culture but also to the iconography of the Orthodox church. You have to study icons to understand the significant way of bowing, which can be explained as the result of historical suppression. It is not only a way of praising God but also a way of expressing slavery, helplessness, and a way of expressing human fate. This is in contradiction to the Western model, where everything was built on the pride of the individual.

In the Eastern tradition you always belong to someone or something. Somehow you are enslaved. Of course, the final author is God, but he owns you. And people own others. The body rebels because suppression forces it to submit to something else. This creates a contradictory act – the head is often raised, the eyes revolting against the posture that the body is forced into. This contradiction is strange – between readiness to submit and resistance, under and above.

Within traditional Orthodox terminology people didn't talk about 'painting' the icons; they talked about 'writing' the icons, or 'scripting' them. This is so strong and significant because it suggests the icon is a written text. The artists *write* an exclamation, a prayer, a lamentation, a challenge to transcendence, to eternity. They are not painting. To paint is to reflect something that is somehow passive, a passive state. To write is an active state. It is to appear.

Those pictures are not only religious tableaux. They are also in relation to essential stages of life. They have something you could call an 'outer radiation', but what was lacking (for me) in such pictures was their inner power. I found that this inner force can be retrieved and exposed through animating them, through creating 'sung pictures'.

The tradition of singing in eastern Europe is polyphonic and the aesthetic background of *Avvakum* was the very refined, polyphonic music of Orthodox religion. This polyphony symbolizes the perfect order and harmony of heaven. The tradition is a very old one and it is cultivated in the Orthodox church.

How is it possible that the human being is able to create such a perfect reflection of his dreams? Of his idealistic image of heaven? A world that in reality does not exist. Where are the slashes in the fabric through which you can see the tragic destruction of harmony? This ugly, hellish reality presents a dramatic contradiction to the perfect world of dreams. So I established the polyphonic music, which runs through the performance, and, at the same time, I cut the fabric showing contradictory sounds and actions. The destruction of reality could be seen and heard through the slashes.

The ideal structure

I am possessed by the dream of an ideal structure. This possession is similar to that of Thomas Mann's Dr Faustus, who was searching for the ideal structure of musical composition. I have been looking for the dramaturgy that will reflect this dream. This ideal structure is close to ritual. Ritual structure is about timing. It is the process of developing the line of life of the event, which drives you through the rites of passage, from initiation to catharsis, and is redeemed by expressive means.

When I worked on *Avvakum* I looked for such an ideal structure. I searched and tried to discover which sort of rituals are the most representative. In the East it is the religious ritual – a ceremony, a mass. I am not referring to religion, I am just speaking about a certain performance, which was sublimated by the centuries until it got its structure, dynamics and composition in the form that it appears today.

'In the distance of hands touching'

There was a significant moment that occurred when I was working on *Avvakum*. We took part in a ceremony in Regietow, a very small village in the Łemko area. People were going in and out of the building because it was Easter, and they walk three times round the church. In fact it was not a church but a room. The iconostas was a piece of material, which divided the room: the kitchen from the social side. The choir was somehow squeezed onto a shelf. Because it was such a tiny church, it was overcrowded and people were compressed together like a thicket. Everything that happened there was so unbelievable: vibrating, touching, energizing. Because all the performative acts were directly person to person. They were in touching distance of each other in this throng. All the stages, sequences, procedures, sounds, songs and candlelight generated enormous energy, which was so turbulent that it seemed as if it were 'The Last Judgment' or a painting by Bosch in which the number of incidents is uncontrollable. This event simultaneously enraptured and devastated me.

In the eye of my imagination I saw all possible theatres at once; the theatres which are the most important ceremonies of our lives and which take place in our homes: baptism, the first communion, the first day at school, the family wedding and the first death. All these events happen in a crowded reality, in a 'dense reality'. When people are so close, in a physical sense, then something fundamental happens which touches love and death and pain and laughter and crying. People are within the distance of touching hands and all the theatrical performative events which have to happen, occur. It is not only a crowd expressing their emotions. It is a performance.

I remember the death of my first love when I was fourteen years old. We were watching the coffin and the room was overcrowded for twenty-four hours, and things happened in a ritualized way: the father's sequence of crying, the mother's sequence of crying, the dressing of the coffin, the moment when we had to leave, the moment when special food was served. Everything was 'dense reality'.

In the image before my eyes, 25,000 years ago, when people were meeting in tiny spaces, in caves, they acted out their fears and had their procedures for doing so. And they gained courage because they'd been together in close proximity, receiving their purification because of this *closeness*. They were *in the distance of hands touching*. I found that – at least for these people in the Regietow church – this crowded room was the perfect space for the perfect ritual. Absolutely perfect theatre.

Later on I discovered the dithyramb – in the period before Thespis – which echoed this situation. The first theatre ever played in the Mediterranean tradition was at the table and people were singing, gesturing, dining. From time to time somebody leaped onto the table to act out a sacred dance.

I had to create a 'dense reality', and the experience in the Regietow church had to be transmitted into the performance. That's how *Avvakum* was created, with the actors as the common body together with the audience within the 'distance of the hands touching', incorporating a large number of very dangerous physical actions, operations, procedures and moves. But there always has to be something which fills this crowded space, which makes a ringing sound that can be heard far away, and this is the music, the song.

I also stress the importance of what I would call 'the closeness effect' in performance. When you are dealing with indigenous people, their attitude is not only to see and to interpret, but their attitude is to see and then to receive proof. What they see is the same as that which they touch. Like Doubting Thomas, who put his fingers into the wound of Christ. I think he was great. He is badly treated because he was seen as the one who didn't trust. No, he was the one who trusted very much, but he wanted his eyes to correspond with that which his body told him. He was more trusting because he wanted to experience much more deeply than those who only saw.

In theatre performance all the images should speak to each other, in the way that musical motifs correspond to each other within a fugue. Create an appearance of chaos and then orchestrate it perfectly. So I do not say, 'This is the story of a seventeenth-century figure, his name was Avvakum, he was a monk, a priest, and he revolted against his hierarchy, the sociopolitical system.' It is too poor, too simple.

When our lives are given as linear narrative exemplar, they are not significant. In this context, we are not significant. But as revelations we are significant. What is revelation? It is when you see an exploded human being suddenly scattered in a thousand pieces.

On the stage you represent a pure being, bombarded by the reality that he causes and the reality that creates him. You see friction, a fight, an *agon*. At these moments, certain parts of yourself can be reflected in those beings. So you can read clusters of yourself. We are living in melodramatic times. There are no heroes any more – none of those figures who represented their times with all the complexities of their world.

Significant moments

The performance of *Avvakum* was built from significant moments, which I took from his autobiography. Let me give you an example. The moment when Avvakum is in court ends with the exclamations of the bishops, 'Seize him! Seize him! Throw his body into the ditch!' This moment of confrontation between the hero and the officials, in front of a hostile crowd, is a point of crisis. He confronts the court, which represents the official religion, society and empire. This is a catalysing moment because each of us, with our own ideas, at some point confronts a hostile world. This is also the moment when the world is corrupting our ideas. We may start to compromise; otherwise we will be rejected, be the loser, be treated as mad. Sometimes this confrontation is inside our consciousness.

Avvakum was put in this situation, which reflects the problem of a single hero versus society, the personal idea versus the common regulations. He uses all possible arguments, actions, strategies, procedures, endeavours, in order to confirm his belief to the others, and to God. Avvakum employs many tactics: frenetic gestures, exclamations, laughter, pleading and curses as he addresses each individual in his attempt to save his life. His approach to them, and his gestures, his exclamations, his prayers, are a huge *teatrum mundi*. When you are in a situation where you have to win, by whatever means possible, and have nothing else to lose, you not only deeply believe but you may also be right in the face of all opposition. You multiply your means of expression. You increase the potency of your acting.

The chorus: the mob

Within my performances I always show the tension between the single hero and the given society. In one sense this is a historical pattern, where the hero has a special calling. He is a predestined creature that senses and understands life differently to the common society. But I believe very much that this is our main problem today. We are alienated in our inner life from society because our inner model of life is in opposition to that which society respects as the proper one. Somehow, all of us are those heroes who fight helplessly against society. It is not only a problem within totalitarian societies, but within democracies as well.

Avvakum on Gotland, Sweden, 1992. *Photo*: Gardzienice Archive.

A Russian icon – a pattern for body language in the performance of *Avvakum*. *Source*: Gardzienice Archive.

Avvakum.
Below: Iga Rodowicz, Mariusz Gołaj.
Above: Henryk Andruszko, Jim Ennis. *Across the wheel*: Andre Turnheim.
Photo: Zygmunt Rytka.

Preparation for *Avvakum* on Lofoten fjord, 1985. *Photo*: Gardzienice Archive.

Avvakum in the cathedral at Arhus, Denmark. *From left*: Anna Zubrzycka, Tomasz Rodowicz, Susana Pilhofer, Andre Turnheim. *Photo*: Jan Rüsz.

Performance 2: *Carmina Burana*

Love

I would say that you always know what you are losing and you don't know what you are gaining. When you are losing you are idealizing. Love is an ideal. Isn't it paradoxical that it is only in the moment of losing that love becomes the ideal? That's why *Carmina Burana*[31] is about lost idealism.

The performance starts idealistically with the image of the Wheel of Fortune reflecting a world which is in perfect harmony. All creatures have an indispensable harmonic relationship with each other. We don't need to know whether the creatures are good or bad, we just welcome the harmony. Suddenly, all of this starts to deform, divide, break down. Finally everyone is against one another. Conflict breeds conflict. In that moment, the moment of losing, we begin to have the sense of what love might be. We are praying, 'God give me again the same chance'. The moment we are sublimating our regret is the moment when there is a link with those that we have unconsciously been touching before. We only knew that we were in the state of something, which makes us not from this earth. We do not belong. We are transported. That's why when love interferes with the social network, it is always extremely dangerous, because you are not only transported but you are transformed – you are unrecognizable. It's very beautifully described in Shakespeare's *A Midsummer Night's Dream*.

For thousands of years, humanity has been creating symbols of transformation. One of them is the ass. Jesus Christ was symbolized by the ass in the first era of Christianity. The first painting of the crucifixion in the second century shows a crucified ass on the cross. The symbolism is very far-reaching and we know that love transports, transfers and transforms us into beings that are not of this earth. That is why social regulations are so opposed to love in its pure state. This philosophical explanation is beautifully explained in the story of Tristan and Iseult.

When I am asked about my political perspective, I say that any system which condemns love is a system which I oppose. Systems exterminate love.

I was drawn to this theme in 1990 because of the common atmosphere. I never believed in history until 1981 and the foundation of Solidarity, because we Poles had been in such a cave, a prison where everything had been suspended. Nothing was real: not politics, history, people, not life. The strongest reality for me, at that time, was science fiction. I was a possessed reader of science-fiction stories. Time had been suspended.

A certain way of thinking brings us to see a performance as not just an interpretation of life, but as a model of life, which has to influence and interfere with its surroundings. Suddenly all these historic processes occurred, and I understood how much of what had happened influenced me. So in 1990 we were in an elevated frenzy, although we didn't know what the future would be. This frenzy was a huge emotional bundle of good feelings, wishes, dreams, beliefs, expectations – and all of these are attributes of love.

We know more about the attributes of love than love itself. It is the same with God. Today people know about the *attributes* of God but not *about* God. Everything which concerns spirituality and beliefs is so confused because anyone can find another attribute and say that really represents the idea of God. It is the same with love. I found myself in such an elevated state that I wanted to deal with love, but I already knew that this perfect picture of harmony would fracture, corrupt, corrode and destroy. That's why the end of *Carmina Burana* is so tragic.

I have already mentioned the beginning and end: harmony to disintegration. I wanted the harmony and disharmony to be involved in the process of the work. The moment you are in dissonance is the moment when you are beginning to understand what love is. And that's why it is necessary to sublimate the disharmonious in yourself to get the full impact of something which you lost.

The legend of Tristan and Iseult is a perfect model to the *Carmina Burana* codex[32] as it reflects the Middle Ages' beliefs and dreams concerning a harmonious world. In 1989–90, we believed the world was turning into something better than before. Somebody declared the end of history and some people believed that we were in transition to another, better, more human, less hostile world.

The world we had been living in was a condemned place. It had been described as an empire of evil. The opposite to a world full of hatred is one full of love. I was looking for a historical reference point where such an explosion and such hope had already occurred. It happened in the early Middle Ages. Or, at least, mythology tells us this was the time of such expectations and projections. It is from that time we have the Arthurian stories, which were constituted on the ideal belief in love and harmony. A little later we have the *Carmina Burana* codex, which is full of poems, songs and prose expressing the human belief in the concept of love. The mythology connected with St Francis and the goliard tradition follows.

There are indicators that the world at that time was not so idealistic, but we also have indications that the world was in a permanent state of fermentation, which directed people to searching (and conquering) love. One of the most significant documents to survive is the story of Tristan and Iseult, which concerns the essence of love and the human imagination in an ideal world. This reflects a certain formation within the history of human culture at that time.

This is not a story, as some would have it, of a triangular relationship which ends tragically. This is a story about the effort to resolve a situation in the most experimental and challenging way. The system made a great effort to marry opposites. We must not project contemporary thinking on to that time. That's our colonizing way of being. That's why the wrong training poisons us within our civilization because we want to possess history. 'We shall say how those people should be living at that time! We should teach those Greeks how to feel, how to think and how to run the world!' That's our *invalid* mentality. Everyone has the potential to be a hero because he or she has their own archetypal model of life. This inner, dreamed model of our life is in total conflict with the model imposed by so-called systems and the society which supports it. We must discover how mythology and history could project on us, and not the other way round.

The basis of the story is that King Mark loves Tristan and Tristan loves King Mark. Tristan falls in love with Iseult. He brings her to King Mark, King Mark marries her. They love each other, but the love between Tristan and Iseult can not be extinguished.

The protagonists of the story made an outstanding effort to marry opposites: to harmonize the conflict. There is an absence of hatred and evil except for one figure – the dwarf. This creature symbolizes disharmony. The dwarf is polluting the environment with poisonous rumours. He gains the ears of the opportunistic, self-seeking barons – the power-brokers. But Tristan, King Mark and Iseult are trying to find a solution within their triangle, because each understands that they represent the constituent life force within this world. When King Mark captures the lovers in the forest, he does not take revenge. He replaces Tristan's sword (which lies between the sleeping lovers) with his own, to show that his intentions come from a source of love and understanding. At the same time he maintains his own authority. Love can be protected as long as three opposites remain in balance: legal authority, phallic power and female honour. And they must be sealed by an oath of renewal.

The symbolism of the sword is very rich. The naked sword between two lovers symbolizes sexual purity but is also associated with phallic power and renewal of an oath. Through this symbolic gesture, isn't King Mark transferring his masculine power to Tristan?

The story of Tristan and Iseult belongs to the tradition of Arthurian stories. That is why I was able to introduce Merlin and Vivienne into the performance. In one version of the Tristan story, it explicitly says that King Arthur and Mark meet each other. The Arthur, Guinevere and Lancelot story is similar to that of Mark, Iseult and Tristan. The model is repeated. The story is not just about a love triangle but a system which is represented by different sides. In that world there is an enormous effort to create perfect harmony. I believe that the story's source is Gnostic. In my performances, I am dealing with human allegories. These characters have symbolic meaning, which suggests a larger perspective.

Incidents

Tristan's madness was presented in the performance. This is the sequence in which he comes to the court as a lunatic and he is not recognized. It represents one of the most critical moments in Tristan's dramatic quest,

when the most idealistic images are expressed in words. He is asked
where he would take Iseult, if she was given to him.

> The King said: 'Fool, if I gave you the Queen, where would you take
> her, pray?' 'Oh! Very high,' he said, 'between the clouds and heaven,
> into a fair chamber glazed. The beams of the sun shine through it,
> yet the winds do not trouble it at all. There would I bear the Queen
> into that crystal chamber of mine, all compact of roses and the
> morning.'[33]

The authors of the myths were perfectly conscious of the fact that
idealism can be transformed into its opposite quite easily, and that the
madness represents a dissolved reality – the other side of the ideal paradigm. Perhaps madness is a harbour for individuals. It does not necessarily signify uselessness or expulsion from society. Madness can function
like a trickster in the tribal tradition. The mad person is the one who
knows more and feels more, possibly because he experiences more
and is able to see further. The entire world is falling apart because love
cannot be sustained. Tristan's madness represents an aspect of this
disintegration.

Merlin is the figure that is responsible for the act of creation – a
demonic figure. In my performance he tries to keep this world under
control. It seems an impossible task. Through his strength and power, he
tries to fill every vacuum. Merlin's is an enigmatic and mysterious story
because no single allegory or figure can guarantee to sustain the world,
and the story tells us that love is the only thing that can. If there is no love,
there is no other power that will keep the world in harmony. From a
realistic point of view perhaps Merlin is making mistakes in his act of
creation. Maybe he creates too dense a reality and the air is filled with too
many existences. Perhaps it is simply a lack of love between all the powers
and all the elements.

Merlin, King Mark, Tristan, Ivan the leader of the lepers, Iseult . . .
they all are in constellation. They are pure representations of powers in
balance. Vivienne is the double of Merlin but she destroys the balance. He
reveals his secret to her and she betrays him. An act of dissonance. Everyone has to live somehow, so they are multiplying their existences. If they
are adequate, they will not destroy the harmony. Sometimes they can

create dissonance but this is an entitled act within the main act of creativeness because it will always lead to consonance.

Embellishing the story

I introduced a local villager into the performance together with a horse and a pack of dogs. Why not? I bring allegories from nature. Merlin represents the element of creation, King Mark represents the allegory of the State, so why not bring another representation which was present in everyday life in the village where we made the performance?

Imagine Beroul the monk, whose task it was to write down this story, which had been told from generation to generation for 500 years. This popular story was in the mouths of the people. Wherever you went you heard this story, and each version is a little different and every storyteller invents his own piece within the pattern. There has to be story of the three key figures, there has to be the Forest of Morois, but not necessarily Dinas, the Lord of Dinan, for example. So every storyteller introduces a lot of other creatures, mainly from his daily environment, because that's the way to bring the story to life.

The trick of actualizing the stories is through introducing interludes, which are creatures, suggestions, allusions and references from daily life. In the story preserved by Beroul, this technique is used when he says that just five years ago a similar story happened in the court of King Arthur. It's the echo of the oral story. So it was with my version of Tristan and Iseult. I heard similar stories when I was a child with the same allegories and problems and complexes.

Imagine poor Beroul, who was given the task to write the story down. He collected all the versions, sat in a cold cell in a monastery and tried again and again to tell this story, and he became obsessed. He did not know which was the best version or how to fill this world with an additional creature when the reality was already so dense. There are dozens of existences. Should we see Iseult in her own country? Why not describe Ireland? What about all the people found there? The Jews were living there at that time. He had to make a selection. He slept through the night and all these creatures knocked on his head, eating his mind, his heart and liver. At the very end he had to make a choice, and thirteen centuries later, I say, 'Poor monk – he made the wrong choice! He didn't introduce the peasant, the horse or those dogs who are actually partners of Tristan when he metamorphoses into madness in the story. Why didn't he introduce Merlin? Merlin was the real demon of this model of life. Merlin was on everyone's lips at that time, anyone who began a story in the pub, on the road, on a pilgrimage to Palestine would start and end with Merlin'.

In building theatre performances, you build a model of your given life. You pick up ideas from wherever possible, but within the given formation. You bring creatures from another reality, but they have to be adequate, and you build a new model of life.

The Wheel of Fortune. *Source*: Gardzienice Archive.

Carmina Burana. *From top*: Tomasz Rodowicz, Grzegorz Bral, Dorota Porowska. *Photo*: Krzysztof Furmanek.

Carmina Burana. *From left*: Mariana Sadowska, Marcin Mrowca, Ilona Zgiet. *Photo*: Peter Widen.

Performance 3: *Metamorphoses*

Childhood

The performance of *Metamorphoses*[34] deals with antiquity and therefore with childhood. 'Childhood' is a better term than 'archaeology' but childhood indicates archaeology, because in order to deal with antiquity you have to undertake archaeological work. You must travel much further with your process of understanding because there is such a distance, the culture is so far away from ours. So somehow you have to dig.

Childhood is the same: when you are older, this process of excavating your childhood can be a big discovery. Some artists, when they are very young, are able to understand instinctively and to transform that which is contained in so-called childhood. Not the childhood when we are small, but the one we inherit from our ancestors. The most phenomenal pieces of art are those made by artists towards the end of their lives who make an effort, undertake a journey to the depths of this archaeological process – for example, Thomas Mann's novel *The Chosen One*, which was the most youthful novel he wrote.

To remember childhood is equal to remembering antiquity, and somehow to 'identify' is crucial here. When you say 'identify with your childhood', it doesn't mean be a small boy, but to try to re-vive, re-draw from the depths of your soul, from your sub-memory. From the depths of your heart that which you inherited when you were born and which is immediately overthrown, overwhelmed by education, by civilization. The stones are thrown on the grave of your inheritance. It happens immediately.

Antiquity

When you are a child you have a natural relationship to antiquity. The problem is, you don't know it, you feel it. Everyone has this ability to travel through the centuries and to travel in his or her imagination, through the epochs.

As children we dream in this way but at that stage we don't have the means to re-create it. You don't know whether you'll be an artist when you are a child (although I believe that everyone is an artist). That is the problem of education today. Education lost that which was most important for the ancients — in those times there was always art, because religion was art, ritual was art. Everyone was involved.

The ancient Greeks inherited everything that came from the sphere of nature. They were in direct relation with this sphere which we alienate from ourselves today. It was the pre-maturing period — childhood. In the context of their theatre, the Greeks were able to express their thoughts through a very light, easy, childlike form. This is a risky term, but I would defend it because we think of ancient theatre as something very heavy, very structured, and very consciously created as a pattern, which should speak heavily through the centuries. Why is it like this? Because the remnants of ancient drama are structures based on words. However, the main means of expression, which was at least of equal significance to the words, were dance and music. Mainly music, but also the relationship to nature because the Greeks always played with it, as in a natural gathering.

Past and present

The main theme of Apuleius' *The Golden Ass* is that of the hero who is transformed into a donkey, and at the final moment is changed back to a human shape on a higher spiritual level. It is as important now as it was 2000 years ago, it is as important now as it was to Shakespeare, to Cervantes, and to many others. This motif returns us to one of the fundamental questions of humanity every time we pass from one system to another, from one shape to another — historical, cultural, and so on.

On the eastern border of Poland, the Soviet Union was once our neighbour. Now it is the Ukraine. Things have changed rapidly in eastern Europe, and history is very close to us. We have entered a new millennium by going through a monumental period of world history. In five, maybe ten years, nobody will remember communism, except for us. It will remain our main source of being, of dreaming. This is how we retain our past, our 'childhood'. Now, at the beginning of this millennium we know that we are still in the middle of a transformation, which is similar but possibly even more difficult than the one that took place 2000 years ago when the ancient gods were thrown away and one new god appeared. ❖

After *Evening Performance*, 1980. *Sitting from left*: Tomasz Rodowicz, Sergio Hernandez, Anna Zubrzycka, Mariusz Gołaj. *Standing from left*: Jan Tabaka, Włodzimierz Staniewski, Elżbieta Majewska, Krzysztof Czyżewski, Jan Bernad, Piotr Borowski, Henryk Andruszko, Sandro Mengali, Wanda Wróbel. *Photo*: Gardzienice Archive.

❖ Metamorphosis and antiquity

(*From post-performance speeches recorded at La MaMa Theatre in New York, 2001*)

In 1987 I invited Jo Chaikin to Poland. It was just after he had suffered a stroke. I asked him to read his beautiful poem 'War in Heaven' in church for the public. We were under martial law at that time – it was a very dark situation in Poland. Jo was very fragile, almost unable to speak. He stood in front of his writing and as he spoke he was trying to *retrieve* the words from the poem – as if he was defrosting the life of the words.

The ancient Greek world also suffered a stroke and it occurred at the moment when Christianity arrived. It is still in this state – we find that many parts of antiquity are paralysed. For instance, we don't know anything about the music of the ancient Greeks because the remnants, which have been preserved, are very few. Small excerpts have survived, found on fragments of papyrus and inscribed on stones amongst the ruins. So, in order to work with antiquity one has to somehow retrieve the texts – of the music, of the movement, of the gestures. One has to retrieve an elementary alphabet. ❖

❖ Retrieving the past

The Vase François was one of the most beautiful objects found in Graecia Magna. It was taken to the museum in Napoli. There was a night watchman who spent his life guarding this vase. Night after night he watched this precious object and eventually he fell in love with it, like Pygmalion with his statue of Galatea. He became quite passionate about its beauty and the myth inscribed on it, which depicted a time when human life was entwined with the life of animals and plants. He grew so passionate that he became possessed, suffering night after night, more and more. He was the only one who was allowed to touch it. Then he allowed himself to hold the vase in his arms. On a certain night, the vase slipped from his hands and shattered into pieces. This precious relic of ancient history was destroyed in one moment. It was then that the people began to really take notice of it. How should they put it back together? And that's the story of antiquity – not understood until *touched*. It is like the ruined past, not only of our history but also of our culture.

I want to show you how, from the ruined fragments, we tried to reveal our roots. Through our passion, through our love and through an indispensable will to touch, like the night watchman, we have tried to re-evoke the dreams of our ancestors. If the ancient world exists in our dreams, in our dramas, then why can't the music be found somewhere in the same zone, within the same sphere of ourselves? Why can't the body motions be hidden in some, perhaps, darker spheres of our nature? We have been trying to rebuild the vase – not in a manner of reconstruction, but of reminiscence.

Antiquity was not merely a written language. It was based on primordial gestures, which create tempo rhythms, dynamics, themes, landscapes and communication. We began by finding antiquity drawn from within ourselves: in our physical practice we encountered the first gestures between 'he' and 'she', the first breath, first sound, first tempo rhythm, the first will to come together, to need and then to get away from each other. The way of working on these gestures was always through our physical training based on 'mutuality'. Theatre is concerned with energy. It is concerned with the chemistry between two people. I am convinced that is how the Greeks understood it with this essential mystery of coming to each other and leaving. They were using primordial gestures, the 'gestus' of the voice and body.

Step by step we worked, first drawing on our inner experience and then through touching the evidence of antiquity, through the vases. And we found that the postures on the vases came from a forgotten line of life inside ourselves – the desire to dance. They were not frozen, static postures: these figures are running, spinning, dancing, flying. The vases show the momentum captured by the painters and sculptors. Antiquity is dancing.

There are probably two ways of reading antiquity in reference to ourselves. One way is based on reading the written language, the other on a way of touching. If we base our understanding purely on language then it reveals how little we know. The entire ancient world, which was embodied in its music, is forgotten, is nonexistent. Pure language forces on us a way of seeing and interpreting, which has to deal with the rational and logical, with statements, communication and imposition. The ancient tragedy was sung. If you interpret the music in this rational way you create a sort of rhapsodic theatre, which is declamatory and performed in a heavy, bombastic way. But we have the right to believe that emotion, exclamation and play were not excluded from ancient tragedy.

There are parts in the texts of Aeschylus, Sophocles and Euripides which are difficult for the interpreters. That's why they are often left as written in the original language, or sometimes excluded from the text. All these are exclamative, lamenting syllables – for instance, 'Oi Moi! Oi Moi!' The exclamations are like passwords, keys to a hidden world. These parts were very possibly sung and in those moments all the inner potential – the subtleties of the soul, of the emotions – exploded.

I believe that ancient performances were much closer to the rituals of indigenous people than to a spoken, rational way of staging Greek drama. Euripides was a very fine musician and an athlete, who travelled round the villages drinking with the people of those times – the peasants, the immigrants. He drank with them, heard their songs and combined their songs with his drama. He wrote the music and notated the choreography alongside the words of his performances.

How did we approach these fragments of the musical texts? We tried to retrieve the words from the fragments; then, through the tempo and rhythm – the musicality of the words – we found the dance of the text, which was inscribed in the music but not in the words. We referred to the indigenous people with whom we have been working. We visited the Ukraine and the Carpathian Mountains, where they speak and dance their own poetry using an irregular rhythm, which I believe is very possibly the way the Greeks also performed.

When you work with the ancient text in this way, musicality is immediately found.

Why? Because it draws us in to this dangerous area of irrationality, retrieving emotions and exclamative acts. When you give out the text, the syllables, the invocation – with the accent not on a closure like 'Amen', but with the accent *on a question* – it creates an uncertainty. It becomes an address to another human being or an invocation, a call to transcendence. The body becomes animated. You have to dance and the voice is sent out, cries out. The ancient Greeks knew what it was for – it served their musical creativity. And that's how we've been trying to read antiquity: through the analogy of indigenous culture, through the analogy of ourselves, and through the sounds and the hidden music of the body. ❖

Fleeing Kore fifth century BC. *Source*: Eleusis
Museum.

Metamorphoses. Mariusz Gołaj with Elżbieta Rojek, Britta Forslund, Joanna Holcgreber. *Photo*:
Zbigniew Bielawka.

Metamorphoses. Front: Tomasz Rodowicz and Mariana Sadowska. *Behind:* Elżbieta Rojek. *Photo:* Zbigniew Bielawaka.

dramaturgy and text

The paradigm of simplicity

What could be both simple and revelatory in theatre work? Is to see, in the eye of your imagination, a tableau which expresses the given subject that you want to deal with? Or is it to readapt a tableau which exists in life? Or should you draw it from the history of art? Whatever the source, you need to make the tableau sing. When I see several people singing together – for example, the Georgians singing in harmony, and their faces are in mutual relation to each other (not too far, not too close, like Van Eyck's angels) – you see a sort of exposure of humanity, a human clan, which speaks very much about that which is common and that which is individual. This is the first and most beautiful picture on the stage.

I often wonder why, at the moment that the curtain rises, we have so much hope and expectation that something important will happen. Something that will give you hope in the future, and trust in human beings, and a belief that the world makes sense. And I have always been amazed at how striking the actors are when they come to bow at the end of the performance, creating a normal, human community. Maybe the play was a failure, but they come and stand in a beautiful tableau.

In this final tableau you can see that one actor is short and cordial, and through him you can appreciate a sense of gratitude. Another is tall and you can see a contradiction between these two actors, the short and the tall standing side by side. One is the perfect foil for the other. Now look at this woman, how naively she smiles. She is uncertain whether the public likes the play or not. Look at her uncertainty. Look at the guy who keeps a bit behind the others, how pretentious he is,

how unsatisfied and how ambitious. He doesn't want to test his quality
with the others because he thinks he is better. Look at this person who
is willing to step back because she knows that the performance doesn't
work and she knows this is a ceremonial act. She is still honest, yes is
yes and no is no. What a beautiful tableau they make altogether and
what a picture to hang on the wall with which to contemplate the
human tribe.

The art of tableaux is very important. It is similar to painting:
you compose in a way that immediately strikes the emotions and
the intelligence.

Imagine this frozen picture on the stage, seven of them, and then
suddenly they start to sing, one, two, then three together. Then they
separate. But they are not like opera singers, pretentiously over-
expressing their voices. They share, they are in mutuality with their
voices, touching each other, exchanging energy, exploring another
voice, going deeper. Suddenly a voice flourishes because it received an
impetus from another singer. Then they stop singing and there is silence.
It is a good silence, which is not heavy, but light. It lets you ask the
question, 'What about me?' Then they speak as in an ancient Greek
chorus. The tableau is a paradigm of simplicity and it is much more
important than the single actor who comes onto the stage and stands in
front of the curtain and delivers a monologue.

*It is important to emphasize that there are a number of smaller pictures occurring
within a tableau. Changing relationships, stories, actions, facts. A complex picture is
occurring. Not one picture telling one truth, but a number of small pieces, which lead
towards a common theme. You allow us to look at the different elements and then when
the singing happens it changes your experience, the singing directs you to look at the
pictures differently. I was thinking of perhaps one of the best examples of a complex
tableau – Leonardo's* Last Supper. *How do you understand this in relation to the
term 'paradigm of simplicity'?*

I worked with Leonardo's picture in so many ways in *Avvakum, Carmina
Burana* and *Metamorphoses*. A very simple picture of what is 'last' and the
most revelative paradigm of simplicity. People sitting together at the
table. It provokes a big question, 'What then?', and consequently, 'What
now?' It is simple because it reflects what we have always done – sat

together at a table and shared our food. At the same time there is a more complex reality because each character brought their own story to this final ceremony.

Facts

The line of life of a role is like a chain. The chain is built from links. Each link is like a musical phrase, so the smallest dramaturgical part contains all the components, the ignition: the beginning, the development and the conclusion. In life you 'cause facts' and this doesn't mean naturalism or behaviourism. It means that every effort of your body, and of your mind, and emotions, has a structure. Within this structure is a sort of dramaturgy, so the same structure should happen on the stage.

First of all, I ask the actor to clarify what he or she is working with. What are the main means of expression and what are the associated means of expression? Because the given task, theme or subject has to play the necessary number of notes to reach the end of the phrase. I ask the actor how he or she wants to articulate it. If the body is first and the voice is just parallel, then make the body the primary element. If you want to express it through the voice, make the sound primary. All the other means of expression should support the same subject.

Frequently, on stage, an actor speaks the words, clearly explaining through the lines the given message, but his body does something completely different. It is in contradiction. All the other elements are working against the message, the spoken language. Synchronize and compose these means of expression and they will all work to achieve the same purpose. So this link is like a little drama, which has to be expressed clearly by the actor. I count the number of musical 'beats', which time the actor's process. The maximum time within a single link is twelve beats: 1234, 1234, 12, 12, and you are done. Then we analyse it and I ask, 'Did you fulfil the task? Did you make it happen? Did you "cause"?'

You have to define the borderlines, and within them the actor has to work with his or her task. In ballet or in dance this is probably better understood than in dramatic theatre.

Text

I am more in favour of poetry than prose. Poetry is very much about the musicality of the words, Shakespeare, Byron, Mickiewicz, Goethe, Homer and Sophocles. There is the famous Socratic frame in Plato's *Phaedrus* when Socrates is provoked to argue about the subject they discuss and he says, 'Don't you see my speech transformed into dithyrambs instead of everyday speech?'

The musicality of the words, the texture, rhythm is very important. Even if I work on prose, I work on a scenario from the excerpt, which composes the words in a sort of poetic structure. It doesn't mean that the sense of the words is unimportant; it is just a way to recompose them. When language is used in a poetic manner, there are subtexts, metaphors, suggestions, indications, parables that demand from you much more careful and deeper work in looking for the meanings than when you are reading essays or prose.

In Orwell's essay 'Lear, Tolstoy and the Fool', he makes an important distinction between Tolstoy and Shakespeare. He says that Tolstoy accused Shakespeare of using empty baroque language, creating cardboard characters and a lack of historical accuracy. Orwell said that, while Tolstoy might be right, there is one thing that he will never understand – the musicality of Shakespeare's poetry. Because he was deaf to the significance of poetry.

Orwell is saying the reason why Shakespeare's language is so popular throughout the world is, above all, its musicality. The sense of the word is not only in information, it can be hidden. You are struck by the musicality of the phrase and the strange composition of the words and syllables. They arrest your attention and you know it is not only on the surface. Your intellectual apparatus is forced to go deeper.

To hell with the author's context

In the beginning of work on a new performance, the words are rather more a texture that I touch like a musical instrument. I know that a certain book is important, I know what it says, but I touch the texture of the book to start to dance with it. Later on, I find the way to penetrate the intelligence of the words, and not the intelligence of the author. This is very important. I do not consider the author, whereas in administrative theatre they think about what the author wants to say through the text. When you follow that line, it may lead you to believe that the text is worthless. Either that, or you don't know how to read the text and you will only use projections concerning, for instance, the political actuality. Notice how fashionable autobiography is today.

Most contemporary writers are popular because of political fashion, but when I read their texts I don't find the quality and weight that is in a text by, say, Beckett. A good text has its own life, and it is like a creature which lives through centuries. That's the only reason why it survives. The text is like a vase. We don't know who painted the ancient Greek vases but they are texts, beings, creatures. If you have a text of quality, which contains the mystery of existence, then the text is living itself. That's why I am dancing with the text not the author. I ask what is the intelligence behind and beyond the composition of the words.

In administrative theatre there is a tendency to deal with all the contexts which surround the author. If you play the author's context more than the text, you very rarely view the text as an organism. For me, the text is an organism. Nothing else exists. Of course, the text indicates a certain direction, because there are so many things in it that you don't know about. In *Metamorphoses*, there is the antique world; it contains a lot of specific symbols, references, and information concerning that world. In order to get closer to the organism of the text, I have to read more when the text tells me with its finger, 'Go there. Open this secret cupboard and find out, and when you have discovered come back to me, the text, and you will understand me better'. But I do not play with the context. I am living with the text.

Small acts

I choose the most effective events from the life of the character and I build the performance structure in a fragmented way. I choose the extreme moments, which are also the most effective and most representative, instead of dealing with the whole biography. Through these events I build a new model in which everything has to be connected. It is a method that could be called a 'jumping evolution'. Imagine a vase, which is clearly covered in pictograms, but which was broken into many pieces. I pick the most significant pieces from my point of view, which represent the strongest and most effective moments of the life of the given character and construct a new model.

Those effective, critical moments from life are like small dramas. They represent a crisis, and they speak about certain sequences of life. In classical drama you would call this an 'act'. They are very short, as they are in life. They underlie the character of a human being as well as give a sense of existence.

During expeditions, the different ways of composing these small pieces provide the best process for naturalization, because both the people and the circumstances are testing them. The dramatic pieces of the drama can be recomposed. The order can change. A death could be first and it will not change the general meaning of the story. It doesn't have to be linear. The music is also a text and the songs also have to be adequate to the act.

section five | **conclusion**

the future of theatre

Home theatre

You said a great and lost chance to evaluate theatre was through the so-called 'home performances' in Communist Poland, when performances were taking place in churches and in homes.

Yes, in churches as well because they were like home situations. It was the biggest chance for the Polish modern theatre, because it was a chance for total rejuvenation. Personal experience reached a climax in these situations.

Partly because they were clandestine?

Clandestine from a political point of view. And this was very helpful, because everything that is clandestine and potentially repressed always creates a special chemistry. The theatre, with all its ambitions, with all its means of expression, was introduced into the homogenous nest: the home. This place where the family gets together naturalizes the theatre performance in a completely different way. It is similar to our gatherings in the villages, where I say that there is no place for false acts because everything is immediately tested properly by an audience which is not administrated. It's like surgery. If the theatre would continue this, like a sort of purgatory, it would develop a completely different morality and methodology of acting. My dream for twenty years has been to do these gatherings in the city, in family homes.

You are saying that theatre has a much stronger impact in an informal, semi-private situation than a formal, public one. And theatre has been in a formal situation for as long as we can remember. The implication of that is very exciting for the future of theatre.

Yes. The future for mystery is to remove theatre from its own venue, and the only place that I see for it in the city is in the home.

Theatre in total democracy

What will be the future of theatre? It is commonly agreed today that our psyche is strongly rooted in antiquity, in our past. But we are entering a brave new world. All that we understand as culture will be reduced to an exchange of information. In a culture of economy, everything is judged by whether it is useful or not. But culture is based on so-called 'useless' things. Culture is the margin in which the human being can re-evaluate or recycle that which seems to be unnecessary from an economical point of view.

Culture retrieves the hidden aspects of nature. Will there be stories of faraway lands, heroes, journeys? I doubt it. It is very possible that culture will disappear as we understand it now. There will only be information, because the media reduces the scale of stories to encyclopedic information. Either useful or useless. Will we have human acts that surprise us, that shake our emotions and imagination? I don't think so because everything will be regulated. Look at Orwell. Was there any place for culture in 1984? In Francis Fukuyama's book in 1992, he prophesied the end of history. It was not necessarily accurate for now, but maybe it will be so in the future. When there is no history there is no mythology. There is not a place for a human being to be recognized as anything other than just a number.

Even now, when people go to the theatre they feel alienated. It no longer restores their memory of the reunification of human kind. Perhaps, like clandestine theatre in Poland in the 1980s, there will be chances to corrupt our perfectly organized civilization. Maybe there will be oases of activity which will be recognized as necessary. Culture will go underground. Theatre will remind us of how it is possible to sing, speak and move in another way; to express extreme emotions and to reach a catharsis which might create a fermentation, even revolution.

Surely democracy will mutate into a totalitarian system and we will have 'total democracy'. Perhaps, in the future, theatre groups will function like partisans, guerrillas that can revoke this perfect civilization.

That was how it was with small theatre groups functioning in the Communist Eastern Bloc. They presented a certain danger to the system.

Theatre is able to reveal all that belongs to human belief, hope and love. Within a controlling system which organizes people and prescribes limitations, theatre will reflect nostalgic patterns of how people used to behave, think and live.

There are two types of theatre – orthodox bureaucratic theatre, and another which is genetically different. It is not a propagandist theatre, but one from the past. Let's think about this theatre which creates models of life in opposition to orthodox structures, or ones which are alienated. This inclination to create another model of life makes theatre very unusual because it deals with the textures of nature which are not normally recognized. For instance, it may be stylizing human thoughts beyond your own thoughts, or dealing with the human body, stimulating a different understanding of it. More than this, it offers a deeper way of hearing, of seeing and experiencing the world. This theatre deals with the chemistry between people, with material which is prohibited by orthodox society. This theatre is an oasis, a cave, an asylum. I believe it will survive.

notes

1   From the publicity programme introducing Gardzienice's 2001 perform-
    ances at La MaMa Theatre, New York.
2   This term was formulated by Leszek Kolankiewicz in a speech entitled 'On
    Gardzienice', presented at the International Theatre Meetings, Warsaw, 1988.
3   See Filipowicz (1987: 162).
4   For more detailed discussion on the student theatre movement in Poland,
    see Cioffi (1996).
5   As quoted in Allain (1997).
6   As quoted in Schechner (2002).
7   Extract from Staniewski's unpublished diaries.
8   See Cioffi (1996) for further discussion on audience responses to
    Gardzienice's early performances.
9   See Hodge (2000: 232–9).
10 Staniewski relates his broader notion of 'musicality' to the Pythagorean
    concept of the *Harmonia Mundi* – the 'music of the spheres'. This
    cosmological concept also interested the Renaissance humanists.
11 For a detailed discussion of mutuality, see Chapter 8.
12 See Rodowicz (2000: 28).
13 See Hodge (2000: 231–44).
14 Sarah Kane, British playwright, born in 1971, who committed suicide in
    1999.
15 See CD-ROM: 'Expeditions and gatherings' @ Time Code: 11.11
16 Second century AD Greek writer, one of the significant literary figures of his
    period.
17 See note 15 above.
18 *Gusła (Sorcery)* was Gardzienice's second performance, first performed in
    1981.
19 Mariusz Gołaj has been a leading actor with Gardzienice since 1979.
20 Adam Mickiewicz's classic play, *Forefather's Eve* (1823, 1832, fully staged
    1901).
21 The Łemko people live in southeast Poland. Gardzienice's first expeditions
    took place in 1981.
22 See CD-ROM: 'Staniewski in conversation' @ Time Code: 2.12, and
    'Demonstration of practices' @ Time Code: 50. 38.

23   See Staniewski (1993: 10–11).
24   Grzegorz Podbiegłowski, company member.
25   Mariana Sadowska, Ukrainian actress and singer, company member 1992–2001.
26   See Staniewski (1993: 25–6).
27   See CD-ROM: 'Mutuality composition' @ Time Code: 55.38, and 'A sequence of mutuality leading to iconograms' @ Time Code: 62.12
28   See CD-ROM: 'A Sequence of Mutuality Leading to Iconograms' @ Time Code: 62.12
29   Other examples of woodcuts from the period are *Cupid with Lovers in the Garden* from Der Seelentrost, Augsburg 1478 in G. Whicher (1949) *The Goliard Poets*, Cambridge, MA: Harvard University Press, and *Ad Ludum Properamus* and *Stetit Puella* from the *Codex Burana* ms. (Codex 4660 in the Bayerische Staatsbibliothek, Munich).
30   See CD-ROM: 'The life of the Archpriest Avvakum' @ Time Code: 16.43 and related texts @ ON AVVAKUM.
31   See CD-ROM: 'Carmina Burana' @ Time Code: 30.26 and related texts @ ON CARMINA BURANA.
32   A collection of secular and religious songs from the thirteenth century found in the Beuren monastery.
33   See Bédier (1965).
34   See CD-ROM: 'Metamorphoses' @ Time Code: 41.13 and related texts @ ON METAMORPHOSES.

bibliography

Allain, P. (1997) *Gardzienice: Polish Theatre in Transition*, London: Harwood Academic Publishers.

Bakhtin, M. (1965) *Rabelais and His World*, trans. H. Iswolsky, Cambridge, Mass: MIT Press.

Bédier, J. (1965) *The Romance of Tristan and Iseult*, trans. Hilaire Belloc and completed by Paul Rosenfeld, New York: Vintage Books.

Brown, D.B. (2001) *Romanticism*, London and New York: Phaidon Press.

Chin, D. (1991) 'Interculturalism, Postmodernism, Pluralism' in B. Marranca and G. Dasgupta (eds) *Interculturalism and Performance*, New York: PAJ Publications.

Cioffi, K.M. (1996) *Alternative Theatre in Poland 1954–1989*, Amsterdam: Harwood Academic Press.

Davies, N. (1984) *Heart of Europe, A Short History of Poland*, Oxford: Oxford University Press.

Hodge, A. (2000) *Twentieth Century Actor Training*, London and New York: Routledge.

Hyde, G. (1992) 'Poland: Dead Souls Under Western Eyes' in Yarrow, R. (ed.) *European Theatre 1960–1990: Cross Cultural Perspectives*, London: Routledge.

Innes, C. (1993) *Avant Garde Theatre 1892–1992*, London and New York: Routledge.

Jaeger, W. (1986) *Paideia: The Ideals of Greek Culture* vol. 1, trans. Gilbert Highet, New York and Oxford: Oxford University Press.

Pavis, P. (1996) *The Intercultural Performance Reader*, London: Routledge.

Schechner, R. (2002) *Performance Studies: An Introduction*, London and New York: Routledge.

—— and Wolford, L. (1997) *The Grotowski Sourcebook*, New York and London: Routledge.

Taranienko, Z. (1997) *Gardzienice Praktyki Teatralne Włodzimierza Staniewskiego*, Lublin: Wydawnictwo Test.

Yarrow, R. (ed.) (1992) *European Theatre 1960–1990: Cross Cultural Perspectives*, London: Routledge.

Articles and interviews

Filipowicz, H. (1987) 'Gardzienice: A Polish Expedition to Baltimore' in R. Schechner (ed.), *The Drama Review* 113 (1).

Foley, K. (2003) 'Metamorphoses is a Gift from Poland' in theatre review section, *LA Times*, 10 March.

Gerould, D. (1986) Introduction to 'Adam Mickiewicz's Lectures on Slavic Literature' in R. Schechner (ed.), *The Drama Review* 30 (3).

Holder, T.M. (2003) 'Metamorphoses: Poland's Staniewski Center at the Getty' in *Entertainment Today*, 28 March.

Kosiński, D. (2000) 'Theater v. Death' in *Center for Theatre Practices Gardzienice*, trans. Thornton, brochure, Krakow: SCRIPT.

Pawluczuk, P. (1981) 'Expedition as a Way of Life' in International Association of Theatre Critics (eds) *International Year Book '80*, Warsaw: Krajowa Agencja Wydawnicza.

Rudowicz, T. (2000) Article in CD booklet, *Gardzienice, Metamorfozy – Music of Ancient Greece*, Altmaster.

Staniewski, W. (1987) 'Baltimore Interview with Richard Schechner' in R. Schechner (ed.), *The Drama Review* 113 (1).

—— (1993) 'Gardzienice, Poland', extended interview with Peter Hulton, Dorinda Hulton (ed.), Exeter: Arts Archives, Arts Documentation Unit.

—— (2002) 'Here One Catches Fire', interview with R. Pawlowski, *Gazeta Wyborcza*, trans. A. Dabrowska, 11 October.

Szybist, M. (1982) *In The World's Circus, Musicality*, Teatr STU, trans. P. Allain, Warsaw: Młodzieżowa Agencja Wydawnicza.

Wildstein, B. (2002) 'Theatrical Meditations and Dionysian Intoxication' in *Rzeczpospolita* 31 August–1 September, trans. A. Ginko-Humphries and C. Humphries, p. A13.

Minimum requirements

- Pentium PC with 20 mb free space on the hard drive

- Soundblaster 64 or compatible sound card

- Speakers or headphones

- Screen resolution set to 800 × 600 pixels

- 16 mb RAM

- Windows Media Player 6.4 or above (available from www.microsoft.com)

Please close down other applications while running CD-ROM